LOVE

One Day at a Time

Collective

Love

One Day at a Time

Modus Vivendi Publishing Inc.

Published by:
Modus Vivendi Publishing Inc.
2565, Broadway, Suite 281
New-York, NY 10025

Cover design: Marc Alain
Page layout: Modus Vivendi Publishing Inc.

ISBN 2-921556-58-8

Foreword

When we attempt to identify the basis for relationships, we quickly see that the couple goes far beyond the concepts of love and commitment. Love and commitment make it possible to share our lives for a little while, but a solid relationship calls for patience, kindness, humour, sharing, generosity and understanding. At times, the list of qualities required to build a relationship can seem staggering. However, in a relationship there can be a synergy that cements two lives together forever, from the moment that both partners decide to share their lifetime experiences.

We are all individuals in our own right. We are self-sufficient, determined and free. So why bother with a relationship, why put our energy in it, why agree to compromise for its sake? Basically, the reason is that we all feel that life as a couple is more enjoyable and a primary source of happiness, sharing and intimacy. The couple is the best possible alliance, a stronghold that gives us the assurance that we have a place in this world. The couple reminds us that we are loved and it urges us to love our partner in all facets and in all states. The couple is a work of art that two people create together — one that remains forever uncompleted. The couple is a solemn pact that we enter into freely with another spiritual and free being. The couple generates and regenerates itself day after day using as its source our desire and choice to be where we are and to experience our commitment.

For my part, I must say that it took several years before I achieved the wisdom and the maturity a relationship requires. I was loved and I loved passionately and intentionally, but I had not understood or found within myself the basic characteristics needed to sustain a long-term commitment. Perhaps I was blinded by the idea that the next relationship would be the right one or perhaps I was simply too independent. Luckily, life taught me well. Today, I live with the certainty that I have chosen exactly the right person.

The Publisher

Introduction

In preparing this book, our goal was to provide a consistent source of inspiration and the tools needed to ensure the growth and the deepening of your relationship. Those currently involved in a relationship can use the daily affirmations and testimonials featured in this publication to improve their lives as part of a couple and to find new sources of satisfaction in such a life. Those not currently committed to a partner may find the strength and the determination to build a lasting relationship.

Love - One Day at a Time is not a recipe book or a rule book, but an exploration of the dynamics of relationships and a series of affirmations that may lead to new awareness. The couple is a place of love, sharing and passion, but it is also a place of work and communication that truly finds its full potential when two individuals choose to look and move forward together in the same direction. The couple is an agreement in principles based on mutual respect and love. Each individual is free. Free to love or not to love, to stay or to leave, to communicate or not to communicate, to respect commitments or to change their minds. Since we are free, the couple is a contractual association in the true sense of the term. The contract is negotiated at the outset and subsequently, may be renegotiated periodically. And because we are free, forming a couple is a privilege, not a right. To maintain this privilege, each day we must work at being together, we must choose to be together.

On the following pages, together we will explore what life as a couple is all about. How can we deepen this most important of all human relationships? How can we learn to live together in joy and harmony every single day? How can we achieve self-fulfillment within a couple and how can we ensure that our partner achieves self-fulfillment as well?

Many people have contributed to the preparation of this book by sharing their experiences, the events that have led them to greater awareness, their techniques, their victories and their failures. *Love - One Day at a Time* is not a theoretical treatise, it is a vibrant expose on the glory and challenge of the couple. Bon voyage!

JANUARY 1

The Dawn of a New Year

"When I met Caroline, I was 36 and I had the impression that I would never meet the right woman. I had just ended a very painful relationship, the latest in a string of failed relationships. In Caroline, I met the woman of my life. Today, we live together and we're very happy. I can't imagine what life without her would be like. I am happy that I chose to stay with her and to work at our relationship. Naturally, I did make some mistakes in the past. But today, I live for the present and I see a very happy future with her. I could end this relationship, as I have ended others, but why should I want to start all over again when life is so good right now."

— PETER S.

Relationships must be reinvented each day and each year. The new year is the opportunity to pursue our journey as a couple. We have lived through all kinds of experiences and we have overcome a number of challenges. We can use this first day of the year to strengthen our commitment by proclaiming our resolve to stay together. We know that despite its ups and downs, life as a couple is much more enriching and satisfying than life alone.

Today, I use the opportunity of the first day of the year to renew my love for my partner.

The Journey

Relationships are never static. The couple is a dynamic undertaking that calls for the active participation of both individuals. The couple can grow when two people who love and respect each other agree to communicate and to set common goals. They agree to travel together on their life's journey, setting out to achieve their common goals. And along the way, they agree to support each other. If we entertain the idea that marriage or a relationship is an end in itself, we are poorly prepared to take on the problems and overcome the barriers that we inevitably find in our path. If we see the couple as a process, we agree that change will be part of that process.

Today, I see that the couple is a process and not a static state of being. I must be present and I must contribute each day to the growth of our couple.

January 3

The Hidden Side of Failure

"When my relationship with Phoebe came to an end, I felt that my whole life had ended as well. I had put so much energy and so much of myself into that relationship! My self-esteem was shattered. For several months, I had very little interest in life and I was going around in circles. Little by little, I began to rebuild my life and the pain began to dissipate. When I met Laura, I told her that I wasn't ready to open my heart to a new relationship just yet. She was patient with me. With Laura, I learned how to love and how to let someone else love me. Laura wanted to work with me to restore my desire to be part of a relationship. She helped me accept the failure of my previous relationship."

— Robert L.

Behind each "no" there is a "yes". Behind each "failure" there is a "victory". We can learn much more from our failures than we can from our successes. Behind each failure lies all that we refused to understand, all that we refused to accept or face, all that we refused to see or hear. When I embrace failure and when I am willing to hear the secrets that it seeks to tell me, I am open to growth and to learning. Today, I know that failure eventually leads to a greater victory.

Today, I see that failure is nothing more than a lesson I must learn. I use failure to strengthen my determination.

Finances

"What I find hard in my relationship is the question of finances. I'd like to be able to buy us all the finer things in life but we both have student loans to repay. We live in a tiny apartment in London and we barely have enough money to make ends meet. We work very hard but half of our money goes to taxes and the rest we need for essentials. Most of our arguments are over money and finances. Marielle would like to buy a few dresses and I am sick and tired of taking the subway each morning. I'd like to buy a car and I'd like to be able to go away on weekends. I can't see when we'll be able to afford any such things."

— LUDOVIC F.

Many couples experience financial difficulties. The important thing is to be aware of the situation and to plan together to find solutions.

Today, I decide to take control of my finances. I know that by working with my partner, we can resolve our financial problems.

JANUARY 5

Small Loving Gestures

"One of the things I like about us is that although we've been together for more than 20 years, we still make those small loving gestures that keep us close. Now and again he brings me flowers for no special reason, just to tell me that he loves me. He phones to say that he loves me and then invites me on a romantic date. When he sees that I'm tired, he runs a warm bath for me and then massages my back. He looks at me tenderly almost every single day. We still touch each other a lot. I like to give him small surprise gifts and I like to prepare his favorite meals. When we're with friends, I like to boast about the things he does well, though I don't exaggerate. For me, these small loving gestures remind me that I've made the right choice and that 20 years later, we're still in love."

— CHRISTINE C.

We sometimes forget to pay tribute to our love with small gestures that say "I love you". It's so easy to touch someone tenderly, to say thank-you with flowers, to celebrate our love by spending a few quiet hours together. Too often, we take our relationship for granted.

Today, I pay tribute to our love and I show my love with small gestures.

JANUARY 6

The Joy of Being Single

"My single friends try to convince me that they're happy being alone. They claim that they can do what they want to do, when they want to do it. They are under no obligation, they have no one to report to and they can go dancing until the wee hours of the morning. I think that there's no more miserable or depressing a life than being single. A single person is always grappling with boredom and loneliness. Single people don't feel comfortable in social situations. The people around them wonder what's wrong with them and why they aren't married. I wouldn't want single life. I prefer the stability, consistency and warmth of life as part of a couple."

— JAMES W.

Today, I choose life as part of a couple.

Commanding Respect

"I spent years getting my husband to respect me. He was brought up the old-fashioned way, when women were supposed to be seen and not heard. I could see that despite his outdated attitudes, he was a good and intelligent man. I took the time to teach him to respect me and to listen to the real needs we had as a couple. Today, I can express myself freely and he listens carefully to my needs. I am happy that I was patient with him — my effort paid off in the end."

— MARIE G.

Respect is a crucial factor in a couple's relationship. We must respect the choices, personality and aspirations of the person who shares our life. And we must be respected in return. Many people are so preoccupied with the need for love and approval, they are afraid of self-affirmation. We can be loved and respected. We can teach others to respect us.

Mutual respect is crucial in a relationship. Each partner must have the space and the possibility to express themselves and make their own choices. This aspect of a relationship is so important that a lack of respect will inevitably lead to a breakup or to a lack of genuine communication.

Today, I will listen carefully to my partner's needs and I will ask that my needs be respected as well.

JANUARY 8

Cooperation

"I always thought it would be ideal to work with my wife, in our own company. I'm happy to see that I was able to set up the situation. Karole and I work together every day. I share everything with her and I never get tired of her company."

— MARC A.

Everyone agrees that a couple should set common goals. The lack of a common objective can easily lead to isolation and to an abandoning of the relationship. We must be careful not to wake up one day to the realization that we have nothing in common any more, that we don't know each other any more. Today, men and women are under increasing pressure to build a brilliant career and to set aside the values of family life and relationships. Although not all couples have the opportunity of working together, the projects they have in common are a chance to share experiences and to learn to work together.

Today, I set goals and I organize projects that I can share with my partner.

Choosing

"In the 1970s, everybody wanted to live all of their emotions and to set out for adventure. As feminism became popular, I convinced myself that I was more attracted to women than to men, that I could find more fulfillment in a relationship with another woman. So I ended my relationship with Bernard in spite of the fact that we had two young children. I found all sorts of reasons to justify my decision and to live out my feminist experience to the end. But after a few years, I realized that living in a relationship with a woman involved the same challenges and the same difficulties as living in a couple with a man."

— NICOLE B.

Living in a couple means taking someone else into account. Our choices can have a strong influence on the other person. We continue to make choices, but we must measure the impact our choices will have on the other person. With time, we come to see what the other person accepts or refuses. We come to see how to act in the best interests of the couple. The first choice is being together. Other choices stem from this one choice and must strengthen that fundamental decision. The couple offers a privileged framework since it is the first place where we are called upon to create something along with another person.

Today, I take the time to evaluate the impact my choices have on my partner and on my relationship.

January 10

Romance

"Romance is the champagne and chilled glass of love, it is the magic that has you dance the tango, the perfume you remember, a heartfelt fantasy come to life. Romance is the antidote to boredom, it is the inspiration of passion. As soon as you let romance filter into your relationship, you are instantly elevated to a delightful state of well-being. Simply because of romance you feel beautiful, elegant; life seems full of hope; the moon, the stars and the planets shower you in benevolent light and you believe that anything is possible — your loveliest, boldest, most cherished dreams will certainly come true."

— Daphne Rose Kingma

Today, I embrace romance within my relationship. I look for opportunities to express the depth and sweetness of my tenderness. These wonderfully soft moments will reinforce our ties and our passionate love.

JANUARY 11

Emotional Support

"No one can live his life solely for himself. Thousands of strings tie us to our brothers; intertwined in these strings, like feelings of compassion, our actions are transmuted into causes and return to us as effects."

— HERMAN MELVILLE

I can accept my partner's help and emotional support. It may be true that negative experiences have led me to believe that accepting help and emotional support are signs of weakness and inevitably lead to betrayal and exploitation. In reality though, there are individuals who are worthy of my trust and whose support I am willing to accept. I am open to the help my partner offers me, just as I am prepared to offer my help and my emotional support to my partner.

Today, I readily accept my partner's support.

January 12

Loving, One Day at a Time

The expression "*One day at a time*" was developed by Alcoholics Anonymous, a group that recognized that rehabilitation from alcoholism is something achieved one day at a time and one minute at a time. The individual who is trying to wean himself from alcohol must succeed in getting through one day; looking at a lifetime without alcohol is a thought that may be too threatening or frightening. A day without alcohol is a victory, one step closer to sobriety and control over a powerful dependence.

This philosophy can also be useful when looking at life in a relationship. If we begin to contemplate living our entire lifetime with the same person, with all the challenges and demands this may involve, we may find the idea overwhelming. Instead, we should say: "I am with you today and I will do my best to make this a positive and enjoyable day for both of us." We can find emotional and spiritual equilibrium in our day-to-day lives and to do so, we must be willing to share our lives, to learn to love and to learn to be loved. The notion of living in a relationship one day at a time can help us through difficult times because it shows us that each day brings its own small victories.

Today, I know that I can live in a fulfilling relationship, one day at a time. I can achieve my objectives for personal growth by building a committed relationship.

Accepting Myself Unconditionally

"Gradually, I must accept myself as I am — with no secrets, no disguises, no falseness and no rejection of any facet of myself — and with no judgement, no condemnation or denigration of any facet of myself."

— ANONYMOUS

Being involved in a committed relationship requires that I love myself and that I accept myself unconditionally. A relationship confronts us with a variety of challenges that test our self-love and our ability to love ourselves and others. A relationship can also provide a framework within which two loving people can contribute to each other's self-esteem. By loving the other person unconditionally and with no preconceived ideas, we can help them create a stable identity based on self-love. Small gestures and small words of love and approval serve to strengthen the relationship and each partner's self-esteem.

Today, I will make the small gestures of love that will reinforce my partner's self-esteem.

All the Good Things in Life

"One day I realized that I wasn't happy in my relationship. I felt that I no longer had anything in common with the woman who shared my life. Our relationship had become boring and superficial. And although in the beginning I had truly loved her, now I felt no love at all. So I told her about my feelings, a bit harshly. Ann was upset by what I told her. To my surprise, she wanted to work with me to revitalize our relationship. We put a lot of time and effort into getting close again, into rediscovering who each of us was. Today, I am married to the woman of my life."

— PHILIP B.

We tend to put limits on what we think we can have. In the end, these limits create a feeling of deprivation. The negative attitude that we are unable to achieve a given result or to build an ideal relationship cripples our ability to enjoy life to the fullest. A positive relationship is an essential element in a happy life. We deserve a relationship that we take pleasure in, that brings us personal satisfaction. We can build the ideal relationship, a relationship based on sharing, understanding and cooperation.

Today, I see that I can have a happy relationship.

JANUARY 15

Learning from My Mistakes

"We had been married for more than 15 years when I decided to take a lover. I felt that my husband wasn't interested in me any more and I was getting older. I had convinced myself that by having an affair, I could bring things back to how they had been, that I could make him pay attention to me. The whole thing turned out to be a disaster and it cost me my marriage."

— IRENE G.

We can forgive ourselves for the mistakes we've made in the past. What is past is past. We are here, now, and the entire future lies ahead of us. If we drag the past with us, we are less free to act and to create. So say goodbye to the mistakes of the past.

We are here to learn, to grow and to experience life. So we must accept that mistakes are a part of life. When we make a mistake, we use it to learn and to adjust our aim. Criticism and guilt can accomplish nothing.

Today, I know that the mistakes of the past must be left in the past. My mistakes teach me valuable lessons that will help me in my relationship.

JANUARY 16

Being Open to All Experiences

"With Catherine, I can be open to all experiences. Sometimes she drives me crazy with her strange projects and original ideas. But it all makes life more interesting. Without Catherine, my life would be too routine. I prefer living an odd life with her over going through life like a sleepwalker."

— PETER C.

Today, I am open to all sorts of experiences with my partner. I know that I have nothing to fear and nothing to avoid and I know that I can trust us completely. When we take on life as part of a couple, we can support and console each other. Our relationship exists for us. Our relationship is a warm home in which we can face any situation.

Today, I am open to all experiences with my partner.

January 17

Loyalty

"For me, a relationship is like a hockey or football team. We defend our teammates under all circumstances. The important thing is the team. Together, we can win, or even lose. But at the end of the game, we're together again in the dressing room."

— Alex G.

Loyalty is a vital factor in a relationship. When we agree to become part of a relationship, we agree to support and listen to the other person. The other person is important to us and we are important to them. No person outside the relationship can motivate as strong a commitment or as strong a form of loyalty. The couple is the first, most definitive and most all-embracing pact. My partner expects me to be there at all times. No couple can survive without loyalty.

Today, I pledge loyalty to my partner and to our relationship.

JANUARY 18

Being There

"Tom is an extraordinary man. He saved my life. When we met, I knew that he was the love of my life but I had a dependency problem at the time. I was still managing to control the situation but I knew that I had a problem. Tom was in love with me and I know that he didn't fully understand the extent of my problem with alcohol and drugs. I thought that the stability of a relationship would help me solve the problem. The first years of our marriage were very hard. I swung between over-consumption and abstinence. Tom was increasingly worried to see that I wasn't managing to get full control over the situation. When I had a miscarriage, things got even worse. I fell into a bottomless alcoholic depression. For weeks, Tom had to pick me up off the floor and put me into bed. I gobbled antidepressants as if they were candy and I drank as much alcohol as I could to forget about the day before. Finally Tom put his foot down. He drove me to a detox center and he told me this was my one and only chance. "Sober up or don't come home." I had the roughest time of my life in that center, but finally I came out on top. I haven't drunk a drop of alcohol since and I have taken a single antidepressant either. All this happened eight years ago. Today, we have two beautiful children and I am proud of myself."

— JOANNE T.

Today, I am proud of myself. Regardless of my past mistakes, I am on my way to a better future.

January 19

The Power of Our Dreams

"Richard and I imagined taking our retirement at 45 and sailing around the world. We nurtured our dream for years. When I became pregnant, our dream was shattered. Today, we have a wonderful family and we are happy. I love living and dreaming with my husband. No matter what happens, we will always be together."

— Rachel H.

A relationship is a dream shared by two people. We dream of the future together, we dream of what we want to accomplish together. Every couple's dream includes adventures, a satisfying sex life, progress on the material level. Every couple's dream includes a family, children, personal growth and maturity. The dream of a couple is a dream built by two and something shared every moment of the day.

I can tell you how I imagine our future together and you can tell me how you imagine it. Together, we can imagine an enriching and exciting future that resembles us, inspires us and pushes us forward on life's path.

Today, I see a dream that is greater than me: the dream of a couple. The dream contains our aspirations, our desires and our future together.

January 20

The Road to Love

We sometimes feel that some people enjoy a perfect relationship while others are destined to experience suffering and fear. In reality, any relationship is a labor of love. At times, the labor of love can be hard, at times it can be easier. Of course, some couples experience severe difficulties: lack of communication, domestic violence, dependence and substance abuse. Under such circumstances the labor of love is undoubtedly much more demanding than it is when both partners live well-balanced lives. But all is possible within a relationship because it is a place of love, welcome and healing. Together, we can overcome all obstacles. Together, we can change life for the better.

Today, I travel the road to love with my partner. The road can be bumpy and winding, but it always leads to the profound truth of love.

January 21

Magic Recipes

"My husband began by telling me that he wanted to sleep with other women and that he didn't feel good about himself. We decided that he should consult a psychologist. After a few months of therapy, he announced that he was leaving me for his therapist. Ten years of marriage down the drain! I wondered if psychologists have an official code of ethics and if there were laws against this type of behavior. We had hired that woman to help us!"

— Marian F.-P.

Beware of magic recipes when it comes to relationships. We can always find a few bits of truth in popular psychology books, but these truths will never be sufficient to ensure the survival and development of a couple. The couple is based on an agreement between two human beings who choose to be together and to create a life together. They create this life as best they know how. They live their life as a couple from day to day and under a variety of circumstances. One day, for one reason or another, one of the partners may decide to leave the couple and soon after, the relationship dies. There is no magic recipe to make a couple work or to make it last. The couple consists of two individuals who are convinced that they are and will remain happiest if they stay together.

Today, I renew my commitment to build my relationship step by step, every minute of the day.

January 22

Marriage

"I realize that marriage is a lifetime commitment, but not at any price. I thought that destiny had mapped out the entire road for me in this regard. I thought that once I had met the right person, all I had to do was sit back and let things happen. But life has taught me a different lesson. Marriage is something a couple creates together every single day. Each partner has specific responsibilities to shoulder and specific work to do."

— Daniel B.

An important factor determines the value and quality of a marriage: honesty. A marriage is doomed to fail when one partner holds back certain things or is unwilling to share secrets openly. Secrets, lies and infidelities have no place in a loving relationship. It's as simple as that. A relationship must be based on honesty and transparency.

Today, I recognize the value of honesty in my relationship.

January 23

Here to Love

"When the children left home, our life as a couple changed dramatically. I felt that I deserved to rest, but my wife Angela had another way of looking at things. She wanted to travel, visit museums, take part in group activities. In the beginning, I didn't really agree with her and I tried to get her to slow down. Unfortunately, my efforts were in vain and I had no choice but to adapt to a new and more active lifestyle. Today, I can say that I love our life together. I am happy that she pushed me (and sometimes dragged me!) out of my shell."

— Eric V.

We are here to love and to learn. Such is the essence of my mission. We can accomplish part of this fundamental mission within our relationship. A relationship is a dynamic and living place. A couple cannot exist without love and change. When we are aware that we are here to love and to learn, we are open to every type of experience life can bring us within a relationship. A relationship tests us, it pushes us to go beyond our limits, it leads us to a better understanding of our partner. A relationship forces us to face the challenges of love without fear.

Today, I see that I am here to love and to learn. I can fulfill this most important of all missions within my relationship.

JANUARY 24

Love and Only Love

According to American author Rollo May, "love is an act of will". At the outset of a relationship, we are caught up in the dynamics of passionate love, which leads us to a closeness and then to a fusion. With time our original passion may dissipate and we must bring a new type of dynamic and energy to our relationship. A couple lasts when we choose to love, when we decide that each day we will express admiration for the person who shares our life. Love in a couple is not a feeling, it is a commitment to love long after the energy of initial passion has faded away. A couple is a contract of love that two free people enter into together. We are free to love and to build our relationship every single day.

Today, I see that the love between us must be nurtured every day.

January 25

Tenderness

"Kathleen has a very soft and feminine voice. She rarely speaks loudly. It takes something absolutely abominable for her to speak loudly. Her voice carries a type of tenderness that makes me feel secure, that comforts me. She is a gentle and kind woman. She moves about like an angel on a cloud. Her presence in my life is like an oasis of tenderness and love. I love this woman with all my heart."

— Vincent L.

The couple offers a framework of tenderness, sensuality and romance. The presence of our loved one gives us an opportunity to share and to communicate. We can communicate our deepest and most intimate wishes and needs with tenderness. Closeness and our trust in others can be expressed without holding back. We can let the other person see all of our vulnerability and all of our needs.

Today, I communicate tenderly and kindly. When I do, I create a warm and secure atmosphere that encourages intimacy.

January 26

Responsibility

"We get up at four in the morning and we work in our cafe until seven o'clock in the evening, every day, seven days a week since we serve breakfast, lunch and then light snacks. Not everyone could work this hard. My wife and I come in contact with people every day. We have to be quick, polite and welcoming toward customers. But neither my wife nor I would change our lives. We are together all the time and we're happy. I like to have her with me. We talk and we laugh all day. She is my best friend and the only person on earth who truly understands me."

— Bernard G.

Responsibility is not a burden or a test. Responsibility is our ability to accept, to receive and to have. As we accept full responsibility for our lives and our actions, our confidence and our control over our own destiny will increase.

Today, I see that when I accept that I am the source, the origin of all that I experience, I become responsible; and when I am responsible, absolutely nothing is beyond my control.

January 27

Letting Others Love Us

"My parents spent their lives arguing. I feel that my mother spent all her time shouting and throwing dishes. My father used to tell her to shut up or slamming the door behind him, he would leave the house to drink with his pals at the corner bar. When I was very young I resolved not to live through this kind of relationship later in life. I chose a man whom I can communicate with, someone calm and quiet. I see no use in arguing and fighting."

— Paula A.

Today, I prepare my heart to give and to receive love. I had always found it easier to love than to let myself be loved. This way, I felt that I could stay in control of the situation. But now, I realize that this approach doesn't work. I have to be able to give and to receive love.

Today, I prepare my heart to give and to receive love.

JANUARY 28

A Generous Heart

"My mother was a saint. She showed me what love is and what generosity is. When she died, I felt that my world had come to an end. I think that my father hastened her death with his selfishness, his affairs and his drunkenness. Even today, I resent him for being so insensitive and selfish. Today, in my own relationship, I try to be like my mother and I avoid repeating my father's behavior patterns. It may not be a perfect game plan, but so far it has brought positive results."

— RICHARD D.

Kindness has nothing to do with the fear of not being loved; it stems from a generous heart. We do not show our kindness only because we want others to recognize it. Kindness, love and generosity are the tools we use to improve our intrinsic condition and our relationship with others. These tools exist only because of the suffering and problems afflicting us today. In reality, these qualities are the result of our fundamental goodness. We are fundamentally good beings and we want to do the right things under all circumstances.

Today, I listen to my inner self to hear the voice of reason.

January 29

Pleasure

"Currently, it seems that periodically, we have an inborn need to change the state of our consciousness: through our daydreams, the things that make us laugh, the sports we practise, the projects we focus on, or the simple fact of sleeping the time away. Another modified state of mind and an another deeply-rooted need is also linked to this process: experiencing pleasure and having fun. Many children from dysfunctional families have a hard time relaxing and having fun. The ability to be spontaneous and to have fun is a need and a characteristic of the Inner Child."

— Charles L. Whitfield

Many people entertain the notion that they must be serious at all times. Coupled with this is a feeling that there is a spiritual side to suffering. It is easy to see a relationship between spiritual belief and suffering. To some extent, suffering is synonymous with nobleness. But we must realize that suffering does not necessarily bring about change and it does not necessarily lead to happiness and serenity.

Today, I embrace all of life's experiences and I make room in my life for joy and pleasure. I look for moments when I can play and when I can share my happiness with others.

JANUARY 30

Games

"My life had become a constant fight for survival. I felt that most people were against me and were intentionally or unconsciously trying to keep me from changing. There was no real joy in my life, only a few minutes of peace here and there. My road in life was a hard one to travel. I felt trapped. One day I realized that the feeling came from within me, that it inhabited me. It was not something external to me. I had been playing my own games and I had fallen into my own traps. From then on, I completely changed the kind of game I saw life as being and I changed the way I played that game."

— ANDREW N.

A relationship can be an exciting game filled with challenges and victories or it can be an infernal trap that we both fall into. The choice is ours. When we set the rules of the game together and when we stay in constant communication with each other, we can overcome all obstacles and our life together is a fascinating game.

Today, I overcome all the obstacles that prevent me from seeing our relationship as an amazing game.

January 31

The Power of My Intentions

We sometimes think that our relationship is accidental or the result of a lucky coincidence. But there is always a very precise intention behind our meeting with our life partner. Even before we meet that special person, we have made the decision to open our heart and our lives. None of us chooses the first person who comes along, even if that meeting may occur quickly and remarkably soon after our decision is made. We often underestimate the power of our decisions and our intentions.

We are together not by magic or by chance. We are together because we decided that we would be. In the same way, we are not together in spite of our true intentions or merely out of habit. We are together because we are convinced that we are happier, more secure and more faithful to our true selves by being together. All this is true. All this is good.

Today, I understand the power of my intentions. I have decided to be with my partner and each day I decide to strengthen our relationship.

February 1

Keeping Your Distance

After being involved in a relationship that comes to an inevitable end, we sometimes feel the need to maintain contact with our former partner. The emotional ties a couple builds can be very strong and very compelling. All a of sudden we find ourselves alone, without the continuous presence of someone else. Even when the relationship was painful and tormented, we can find it hard to break off our emotional ties for good. Sometimes it can be best to end a relationship categorically and to refuse all further contact. A definite break in a relationship may be much more difficult when there is joint custody of children. In such instances we must attempt to maintain superficial and cordial contact, limiting the possibility for any intimate or more personal interaction.

Today, I am solidly anchored in the present and my focus is the future.

February 2

Looking at Things as They Are

"For a long time, I refused to see things as they were. I thought that by turning a blind eye to the situation, I could avoid confusion and conflict. My relationship had been over for a number of years, but I didn't dare let myself see it. I liked my lifestyle an I didn't want to be single again at age 40, with two teenagers to take care of. But life forced me to look at the situation as it really was when one fine day, my husband came home and told me that he wanted a divorce, he wanted to start a new life with someone else. I could have woken up long before then and I could have done something, but I just didn't want to dare."

— Joan L.

We must learn to look at things as they are. By looking at things and situations head on, we can take on difficulties and solve our problems. When we see things clearly, we can act logically until a situation is resolved in a way acceptable to us. By learning to see things as they truly are, we become stronger and we break free from our fears. By confronting obstacles head on, we become stronger and less dependent on our environment and on the various situations that life brings us.

Today, I no longer argue and I no longer impose my perception on things — I simply look at things as they really are. Just as darkness cannot withstand light, lies and deception cannot withstand the power of truth.

War and Peace

"We used to argue often, over small things, over bigger things. One day we had an altercation that put an end to all the fighting. I grabbed her by the neck and I slammed her against the wall. I was fed up with her constant complaining and I lost control. When I saw the terror in her eyes, I came to my senses and I stepped back. I knew that I had gone too far. The experience shocked us because it showed us how far we could go. That day, we made a solemn pact not to ever let our emotions get the best of us during an argument."

— ARTHUR H.

A relationship isn't a battle ground where the other person is the enemy. A couple should be a place of mutual help. However, we all know that the stress of everyday life, financial concerns and children can cause enormous pressure within a couple. It is vital to find efficient means of communication. When we are angry, we can say and do things that we later regret. Anger alters our true nature and changes the intensity of our communications.

Today, I see that anger can only hurt my relationship. I refuse to give in to anger. I prefer to step back from the situation and think clearly before I take any action.

FEBRUARY 4

Not Giving Up

"When we set up house together, the problems began. Peter never picked up his clothes, he left the bathroom in a mess and he refused to do any cooking. I felt as if I was his mother and I didn't find it very much fun. I spent my time criticizing him. One fine day, I packed my bags and I went to live with my parents. I loved Peter, but I couldn't live like that anymore. Two weeks later, he called me and begged me to come back. So we sat down and made a list of the basic rules for living together. Since then, Peter really shares in the household chores. When I see that he's beginning to slip back into his old habits, I remind him that I can always visit my parents for a few days."

— FRANCES S.

Living with someone else is like a dance. When our intentions are clear and when we are flexible, we can achieve most of our objectives. In a relationship, letting go means giving up a certain number of preconceived ideas and agreeing to reinvent life with our partner. No one wants to be dominated or forced to change against his or her will. However, we can be flexible and we can adapt to the special requirements of living with someone else in a given framework.

Today, I adjust to the special requirements of living in a relationship. I look at our relationship as a graceful dance.

FEBRUARY 5

Humor

"What charmed me most about Michael when we met was his sense of humor. He could also see the lighter side of a situation. I realized that when I was with him, I spent a lot of time laughing and having fun. He knew how to win me over by using his sense of humor. I knew that living with someone like him would always be a lot of fun."

— SOPHIE G.

We sometimes underestimate the value of humor and laughter in a relationship. When we talk about relationships, our main topics are commitment, responsibility, sex and communication. But humor plays an important part in relationships because it is a type of game, of light communication that relaxes us and makes life enjoyable. Why not have fun laughing together and looking at the funny side of situations?

Today, I want to see the lighter side in every situation. I can laugh and I can have fun with my partner.

FEBRUARY 6

Maintaining a Relationship's Purity

"My friend Martin made me understand something that deep down I knew was true, but that I had never expressed: to experience a positive and lasting relationship, we need to be clean. Secrets and lies, even little ones, eventually destroy a couple. Yet many people still believe that what you don't know can't possibly hurt you. Now I know that what the other person doesn't know can end a relationship. Early in the relationship, I did some things that I knew he wouldn't have approved of. I convinced myself that it was best not to tell him because if I did, he might want to stop me from doing the things I really wanted to do and that I considered I had the right to do. I used this reasoning to the point that I was unfaithful to him. I was caught up in a vicious circle of lies and half-truths. Michael suspected that something was going on and when he found out the truth, he threw me out. At that point I realized that because I had no honest communication with him, I had become completely confused. I had to work extremely hard to get him to forgive me and to convince him to give our relationship a second chance. Fortunately he saw that I was sincere and that I wanted to change. Today, I share everything with him and whenever I doubt, I talk things over with him."

— CARMEN E.

Today, I know that honesty and transparency are crucial to a good relationship.

February 7

Courage

"I had been in a relationship with Paul for a little more than a year when we found out that he had multiple sclerosis. We were engaged and on the verge of making arrangements for our wedding. We were flabbergasted and extremely worried and upset about the news. How would the disease manifest itself? How would the disease affect our relationship? Would our children be likely to develop the disease as well? I quickly realized that there is no cure to this particular disease of the nervous system and that eventually, Paul would be severely affected by it. Some people advised me to end the relationship for my own sake, but I loved him and I felt that he was the man for me. After much thought, I decided to make a commitment and to spend my life with him. In the very first years, we experienced some difficulties. Today, Paul is extremely affected by the sclerosis and he is unable to walk or work. We often go through hard times, but we have two lovely children whom we adore. I feel that I have been faithful to myself and that I have fulfilled an important duty. I have no regrets.

— Marie B.

Today, I will be faithful to myself and to those I love.

February 8

The True Source of Problems

"I realized that I was gay at the age of 12. I spent at least 10 years denying that I felt no attraction whatsoever toward women. Meanwhile, I went out with girls and I tried to overcome the attraction I felt for men. I didn't want to be gay because I was afraid to be marginalized and rejected by my family. My life began when I admitted what had become obvious. Between the age of 22 and 30, I experienced a number of relationships. However, I was looking for something more stable and I wanted more commitment. Luckily, I met Philip and he shared my aspirations. We've been together ever since and we're very happy."

— Michael D.

By recognizing the truth, we can identify the real source of our problems. In reality, a problem surfaces when there is something in our lives that we have not been able to confront directly. By understanding the fundamental nature of a problem, we can solve it. In every problem there is something we refuse to face.

Today, I seek truth in all aspects of my life.

February 9

The Challenge of Relationships

"We were under a great deal of stress when our third child was born. We hadn't planned to have Luke and our two other children, who were eight and 10, felt left out. I hadn't wanted a third child but abortion was out of the question at the time. Luke was a difficult child and he spent most nights crying. And to make matters even worse, he wasn't very healthy. From one day to the next, life became a real chore and more and more, my husband began to withdraw from the family and from me. He spent more and more time outside the home and I felt very alone and abandoned. When our relationship was put to the test, I saw what my husband's true nature was."

— Lynn P.

A relationship is a shared project. When we agree to raise a family, we take on a major challenge. One person can raise a family alone, but the job is much easier when it involves two individuals united by the same goals.

Today, I will be present and I will listen to the needs in my relationship and in my family.

FEBRUARY 10

Tender Moments

We sometimes forget that a relationship is nurtured by small things: hugs, affectionate notes, a smile, a hand on a shoulder. We are convinced that the quality of a relationship is measured on the basis of communication, sex, the accumulation of wealth and social status. But we live in the present, and it is the tender everyday gestures that give our relationship its beauty and its authentic worth. When I take the time to say: "I love you"; Did you sleep well last night? Is there anything I can do for you?", what I'm really saying is: "I'm sure that I'm with the right person, I'm happy with you and I want you to be happy." A couple finds fulfillment in the present and in the reality of each day.

Today, I see that small gestures of love and tenderness can make all the difference in the world.

FEBRUARY 11

Being Right at All Costs

"I was fed up with always being wrong. In his opinion, I was the reason nothing was going right; I was the cause of every problem and every hardship on earth. I told him that if he had to be right at all costs, then he could be right on his own!"

— ROBERTA B.

Today, I am flexible enough to see that sometimes I'm right, and sometimes I'm wrong. Ultimately, I recognize that I can win a battle but lose war. So I look closely at each situation and I refuse to give in to the need to be right at all costs.

February 12

Sharing Projects

"It is indeed true that a couple is two people looking in the same direction. Charles and I lived through an experience that profoundly changed our relationship and our entire lives. We already had a son when I became pregnant with Emily. The pregnancy was perfectly normal, but Emily was born severely retarded. When we decided that we wanted to raise Emily ourselves rather than put her in an institution, we underestimated the work and the dedication involved. I had to quit my job and devote myself full-time to bringing up our daughter. After several months at home, I was exhausted and I felt that I was getting nowhere with her. Despite help from Charles, I was running out of steam. We seriously considered institutionalizing Emily in a group home, but when we visited the home proposed to us by a specialized agency, we quickly saw that this was something we didn't want to do. Charles suggested that he would leave his job and that we set up a small group home in our own house. The government was offering subsidies for this kind of enterprise. Today, we work together and we take care of Emilie and four other children like her. Life may not always be easy, but we're happy and we have each other."

— Roxanne T.

Today, I am open to the challenges and adventures life brings me. I know that my relationship will undergo change and I embrace these changes.

February 13

The Commitment

"In our day, close to 50 percent of marriages end in divorce. Divorce is expensive and very difficult for the parties involved. There are many causes underlying divorce. So to avoid divorce and its disastrous consequences, many couples choose to live together without getting married. I myself avoided marriage for many years; I avoided taking position. I saw something threatening in making the relationship official; to me it seemed like buying a one-way ticket to an unknown destination. We can all find good reasons to avoid commitment. But once I took the step, I realized that my fears were unfounded."

— William P.

Marriage is designed to make public and legal a relationship between two people. The official act sanctioning the relationship involves a contract between the two partners. The contract stipulates that we will stay together regardless, in good times and bad, for love, for protection and for life. Marriage is a ceremony that is an opportunity to affirm aloud that we intend to live and to grow together for a lifetime. The fact that there are divorces and family disputes is not a sufficiently good reason to refuse to get married, if we truly love each other and if we are genuinely interested in growing together.

Today, I renew my commitment for better or for worse.

FEBRUARY 14

A Celebration of Love

"Within each of us, there is an insatiable desire to love, to be loved! The love we seek is much more than the euphoric butterflies-in-the-stomach feeling that a new romance brings: it is also the precious consolation of revealing my innermost self to someone else, of being accepted unconditionally and surrounded with good thoughts. It is the deep feeling of tranquility and peace of mind that comes from an intimate and close relationship with another human being."

— DAPHNE ROSE KINGMA

Today, I celebrate my relationship. By opening my heart and my soul to love and to romance, I open my life to my partner. I want to create a climate of warm and passion each day. I want to light the fires of passion and tenderness and I want to make my partner see how important he or she is in my eyes.

FEBRUARY 15

Forgiveness

"When I found out that Madeleine had been lying to me for months, I was furious. She had begun an affair a few months before and after a while, I realized that something was wrong. I started to ask questions and she continued to lie to me. Finally, I got the story out of her and she admitted everything. As soon as I found out, she ended the affair and she asked me to forgive her. I wanted to punish her for hurting me, but I couldn't end our relationship. It took me months to come to terms with the situation. Today, I realize that I wasn't playing an active part in our relationship, I wasn't present. No doubt Madeleine went too far in expressing her boredom and her frustration, but I had my share of responsibility to shoulder. I decided to forgive both of us and to start over again."

— STEVE L.

Today, I see that responsibility is something we share in our relationship. I can always choose to see what my share of responsibility is in any given situation. When I do, I can understand the situation better and I can take the most appropriate steps.

February 16

The Greater Good

"Fortunately, I've always known the difference between right and wrong. Inside, I've always had a deep sense that points me toward the right path or the right action. I stop to listen and I follow the advice of my inner wisdom. Sometimes life confronts me with difficult decisions. I must choose between my interest of the moment and a better long-term solution. I know that I can make the right decision by applying my principles and my values. I can set aside instant gratification and make my choices based on the greater good."

— Isabel C.

Each relationship has its own needs and its own dynamics. In a relationship, we have to look at the reality of our choices. If we let our impulses of the moment guide us in all situations, we are not acting in the greater good. Each of us can maintain our individuality while also listening to the needs in our relationship.

Today, I know that I can maintain my individuality and I can fill my needs while also listening to the needs within our relationship and the needs felt by my partner. I can make choices that are for the greater good without compromising my individuality.

FEBRUARY 17

Domestic Violence

"You haven't experienced hell until you've experience domestic violence. I lived through hell for eight years, with an alcoholic and violent husband and I can tell you that the situation almost killed me — literally. When I met Max, he was six feet tall with curly black hair, rippling muscles and gorgeous blue eyes that seemed to look right through me. He was strong and frank and for me, it was love at first sight. I loved him madly. In spite of the alcohol and the violence, I couldn't bring myself to leave him, I loved him too much to go. With time, love and passion turned into terror. The first times he hit me, he was quick to apologize, swearing that it would never happen again and insisting that he didn't know what had come over him. He would bring me gifts and he would do everything imaginable to get me to forgive him. As more time went by, the hitting episodes became more and more common and he wasn't as quick to ask for forgiveness. I had become a battered woman, living in terror. I hardly dared to look at him for fear that he would slap me or the children. Fortunately, he never beat the children — if he had, I would have killed him myself. I ended up leaving. I had to run away with my children to save our lives."

— PAULINE M.

Today, I know that without mutual respect and admiration, no relationship can survive. I refuse to be the scapegoat in any relationship.

FEBRUARY 18

My Secret Weapon

"My husband adores my cooking. He likes it when I cook for him. I see how happy he is when I prepare one of his favorites, maybe a delicious vegetable stew with home-made bread and a good glass of wine. Now we know each other better; when I start to prepare special or elaborate dishes, he knows that I'm about to ask him about something that's important to me. He knows that he won't be able to resist. Before I even get the question out, he takes me in his arms and asks me what's up. I know this is an old strategy but the best way to a man's heart is really through his stomach! But the game makes us both happy, so why not!"

— JACQUELINE S.

For a long time women felt exploited, and in some instances, rightfully so. They worked hard to get out of the kitchen and to take their place in society. When they did, many men felt abandoned and helpless. Now the situation has settled down and we can rebuild man-woman relationships and breathe new life into the couple. Each partner should contribute to the other's happiness and well-being. The couple exists to create a haven of peace and love for men and women alike.

Today, I know that I can love and serve my partner without giving up my freedom. I can accept the love and service of my partner without feeling guilty.

Our Sex Life

These days, we hear a great deal of talk about sex, sexuality, sexual techniques and sexual problems. The sex industry is flourishing. We are led to believe that everyone must have frequent sexual relations to experience true fulfillment. If our sexual urges aren't satisfied, we run the risk of becoming depraved or mentally disturbed. Freudian psychology served to shape a new sexual reality, very prominent and very complex. Sex experts, the new gurus of sex, constantly refer to the therapeutic value of sexuality. We live in a world focused on sex, where each person must find a place and a role to play. The overestimation of the value of sex has a direct impact on our relationships.

For partners, the relationship is the last refuge. In a relationship two people who love and respect each other can live out their intimate desires as they see fit. Sexuality is but one facet of a relationship, neither more nor less important than any other aspect of the life shared by two people. A fixation with the importance, the frequency and the quality of sexual relations inevitably leads to dissatisfaction and confusion.

Today, I am happy to experience the equilibrium and stability of a couple. I know that I can fill all of my needs within our relationship.

FEBRUARY 20

The Joy of Love

We sometimes forget that love should be savored. We can savor it when we are right here, in the present moment, open and aware of what life has given us. A relationship requires effort. But we also have to take the time to savor our relationship. We have to find the time to play together, to relax and just be together, even doing nothing in particular. When we focus on the fact that being together takes work and effort, we lose sight of the true nature of a loving relationship.

Today, I take the time to savor the time spent with my partner.

Inside Where it's Warm

"I know that during the month of February, a lot of people feel down and depressed. We found a solution to the winter blues. In February, we take a week off to fly South. Our week's vacation revitalizes us and brings us closer to one another. We spend our days on the beach, swimming and lying in the sun. We made this decision during the first years of our relationship. We spend less money on Christmas presents to set aside the money we need for our February holiday. It's like a tonic for our relationship!"

— MARGORY I.

February is a hard month to get through. In February, summer seems so far away. You can see winter etched on people's faces and daylight is a rare commodity. Fatigue and stress take their toll.

Today, I look for ways of creating an oasis in my relationship.

FEBRUARY 22

Learning to Love Yourself

"What does loving yourself really mean? It means setting aside special time for yourself each day. It mean respecting yourself. Spoiling yourself from time to time. It means discovering your personal talents and giving yourself access to the things you enjoy. It means defending your point of view when you know you have to. It is a daily process you can use to come to know yourself, to be indulgent with yourself when you discover less than perfect things in your personality or your behavior and lastly, it means taking steps to increase the self-esteem you need for your personal growth. Loving yourself means being able to admit to your weaknesses, it means knowing that even if things aren't always easy, you've always done the best you could. When we love ourselves and accept ourselves as we are, we are not afraid of growing, learning and changing. We feel full of life and we have the energy we need to have fun with our families and to take care of our loved ones. And since children learn by example, parents are the best people to teach them what loving yourself really means."

— JUDY FORD

Today, I accept myself as I am and I am not afraid to change.

February 23

Temporary Abstinence

"When I set up my own business five years ago, I was under tremendous stress. We had put all of our savings into the company and we weren't sure that we could make a go of it. During the first two years, I worked 70 hours a week. In the meantime, Helen took care of the kids and held down a job at the national archives. I used to spend all night worrying and mulling over the company's problems. Inevitably the pattern began to affect our sex life. I thought that it had been about three months since Helen and I had even touched each other. But she corrected my calculation: our abstinence had lasted seven months! Helen never lost confidence in me. She kept on loving and supporting me."

— Frank C.

Today, I will be the tender, loving and helping hand for the person who shares my life.

Sharing Responsibilities

"I was really surprised to see Richard's enthusiastic cooperation when our first baby was born. Richard spent hours rocking our daughter, changing her diapers, getting up to see to her when she would start to cry in the middle of the night. I'm married to a wonderful guy who loves kids. What a gem! What a joy! I was afraid that I'd married a typical man who'd be willing to do only a few specific things and nothing else to help out. But Richard does as much around the house as I do. If he could nurse the baby, he would! I really feel that we share responsibilities."

— AUDREY L.-P.

Now I see that responsibility is something to be shared. When I look at my relationship, I understand how important it is to share responsibilities. When I take on too many responsibilities without delegating part of them, I feel burdened. On the other hand, when I let my partner shoulder all of the responsibilities we have, I feel that I am contributing nothing to the relationship.

Today, I resolve to do my share and to work with my partner to establish equilibrium in the sharing of responsibilities.

The Truth of the Moment

"If I am unable to find pleasure in washing the dishes or if I want to get the job over with as quickly as possible so I can sit back down at the table to eat my dessert, I am equally unable to enjoy my dessert! As I pick up my fork, I am thinking about the next task that awaits me and the dessert's texture and taste and all the pleasure it brings fade into the background. I will always be dragged into the future and I will never be capable of enjoying the present."

— THICH NHAT HANH

A relationship should be experienced in the present. At times, it can be hard to forget the past. We feel guilty about past mistakes. But the past is gone forever. What we have is the present and its possibilities. Love is best expressed one minute at a time. Passion, tenderness and pleasure are best experienced in the present.

Today, I can express my feelings and I can live the present moment to the fullest.

February 26

Living with a Complete Stranger

"I chose to live with Paul for all the wrong reasons: he had a good job, he drove a nice sports car, he had standing and he was self-assured. At the time, I wanted to look good and I was convinced that he could give me all of the things I wanted. I thought that I had to choose a man who could bring me the material things I wanted. I became pregnant soon after our wedding. I was still under the spell of my original fantasy and everything seemed to be going along smoothly, I thought everything was perfect. But after a few years, I realize that I had absolutely nothing in common with my husband. He took refuge in his job and I was alone all the time. When I tried to talk to him or to plan activities we could do together, he had no reaction whatsoever. He was miles away. After the birth of our second child, I realized that nothing could be done to salvage our relationship. Time and time again, I gave him opportunities to show me that he knew I existed and to plan things with me, but he still secmed to be somewhere else. Now and again he'd mumble that he understood what I was saying and that things would change for the better. But they never did. After five years, I had no idea who he really was; I was living with a complete stranger!"

— Catherine O.

Today, I choose life. I choose to communicate and to relate to those around me. I want to be in a relationship with a living, whole and conscious partner.

FEBRUARY 27

The Domination of Love

It's easy to see how, in the name of love, some people seek to control and dominate. There are many examples of domination: husbands who dominate their wives; wives who control their husbands; parents who keep their children under their thumbs; parents who become emotional hostages to their children's blackmail, etc. Of course, this is not love, but something darker and selfish. Domination is love being used as an alibi to hide our weaknesses and our emotional dependence.

This type of relationship is very confusing for human beings because they hear "I love you" while at the same time enduring painful experiences. They may come to believe that love is cruel, controlling and hard. But true love is based on freedom, respect and the sincere desire to contribute to someone else's happiness. No one should accept domination in the name of love.

Today, I refuse to be dominated in the name of love.

FEBRUARY 28

Change

Some people say we can change, we can transform our lives into something different. Others say that once you're an adult, your personality cannot change unless you live through a traumatizing experience. There is truth in both viewpoints. First of all, personality, identity, behavior, values, attitudes, and the life choices an individual makes are essentially, the result of learning, of culture and of temperament. All these things can change. But the fundamental being, the spiritual and true being does not change because, simply, it is. In very simple terms, change is the gradual or sudden discovery that the true being within us distances itself from what is not true and not essential.

When a relationship is genuine, we seek to set aside the things that are not essential to its nurturing: preconceived ideas that are obstacles to our love and communication; behaviors that make life more complicated and that create conflict; negative attitudes that do nothing to help us support or appreciate our partner. We set aside all that is not helpful to us and we choose to live and grow together in harmony.

Today, I embrace the person I really am and I set aside all the attitudes and attributes that do not reflect the true me.

March 1

The Power of Closeness

"Through an almost mystical process of osmosis, closeness brings about change. We benefit from the essence of who our partner is through the things we see as possible merely because we are close to that person; we change some of the ways we are solely and precisely because we are close to another person."

— Daphne Rose Kingma

Being in a relationship means "being together". By definition, a couple involves closeness, growing constantly closer to someone else. We share our intimacy, our vital space and our inner life with the person of our choice. While the degree of closeness can vary from one couple to another, it always involves reducing the distance that separates one partner from another. Closeness can result in an almost telepathic form of communication and to an almost total empathy. When we are truly close, we can feel what the other person feels. We are constantly in step with the other person and in this unison, we become more and more alike.

Today, I can share my vital space with my partner and as I do so, we vibrate in unison.

March 2

The Simplicity of the Couple

"When we do tasks over and over again, we begin to recognize the natural cycles of growth and deterioration, of birth and death; thus, we realize the dynamic order of the universe. 'Simple' work is work that is in harmony with the universal order that we perceive in the natural environment."

— Fritjof Capra

There is a form of simplicity inherent in a relationship, something natural in and of itself. I love my partner and I want us to be as close as we can. I see that life is better when I can share it and I seek to strengthen and maintain our relationship. All else is simply superfluous.

Today, I leave complex theories to others. I live as I choose to live. I listen to my heart and I look for simplicity in our relationship.

MARCH 3

Life After Life

"When Jane died, it took me a long time to recover. I couldn't accept the fact that she had gone first. I wanted to die in hopes of finding her somewhere in the beyond. I was so very lonely. Life held no interest for me, it was completely colorless. Only then did I realize how much this woman was a part of me. I felt empty inside and I could see her everywhere I looked. About a month after her death, I dreamt of her. She told me that she was fine and that she was always right beside me. I woke up and I felt her presence in the room. I told her how much I loved her and how much I missed her."

— ANDREW W.

Deep within us, we know that the material world is not the only world. We are spirits who borrow physical bodies for a time. We live through our earthly experience and we build ties. These ties survive beyond our earthly life. When we invest genuinely in a relationship, we come into contact with our partner's true being and we cross the oceans of time and light to come together.

Today, I see that the material world is only one part of our reality.

MARCH 4

Our Moral Code

"What I love about her is that I can trust her completely. Michelle is a woman of principle. When she gives her word, everyone knows that she will keep it. Thanks to her I learned how important it is to have a moral code. I saw to what extent I could trust her. Her attitudes and her behaviors taught me we are more serene and stronger when we apply the fundamental principles of life. And I believe that this is why our life together is honest and completely transparent. We have nothing to hide from each other and we can always count on one another."

— JOHN G.

We should recognize how important values are in our everyday life. Values rest on truths that have always served us well. If we truly want to be happy, we must live according to solid principles and we must behave consistently. Our rules of behavior and our values can be very simple. They guide our decisions and our actions and they pave the way to self-acceptance and the acceptance of others. Our moral code must be based on our experiences, our observations and our own truth.

Today, I see that my values guide me on the road that leads away from Evil and toward the light of Good.

MARCH 5

Two Souls

A relationship is a contract. Together, we define the parameters of our relationship, the conditions for satisfaction, the rules of the game. Together, we find a common ground that is greater than our individual ground. If I change, the changes I experience will have an impact on my relationship and they will have an impact on my partner's life. If my partner changes, my life will be changed because we are so close. I must respect the choices and the individuality of my partner and I must demand that my individuality and my rights be respected.

Today, I agree to grow with someone else. I choose to share my life knowing that my actions have an impact on our lives. I agree to let my partner grow and change within our relationship. I resolve to maintain effective communication, regardless of what may happen.

March 6

Telling the Truth

"You will know truth and truth will set you free."
John 8:32

Telling the truth means speaking of true things, opening our hearts and talking about what is truly of concern to us. It means overcoming the obstacles to true communication, to share who we truly are and to share our most cherished dreams. A couple can survive only in a climate of truth. Lies and secrets sabotage a relationship. The union of two partners cannot survive lies because each person is too close to the other not to detect even the subtlest of untruths. Telling the truth sometimes requires courage, particularly when we have done something reprehensible or when we have betrayed our partner's trust. But the only way to build a genuine and lasting relationship is to tell the truth at all times, no matter how hard that may be.

Today, I see that truth and truth alone can set me free from my inner turmoil and lead me to acceptance and forgiveness.

MARCH 7

The Architect of My Relationships

"My love relationship began to truly evolve and move forward only when I decided to make a true commitment. I was always afraid of saying: "Yes, I will stick with you until the very end." I was afraid to feel trapped. I believe that our life together would have been much more fulfilling if I had taken this position much earlier in the relationship. Luckily for me, Gerald was patient. He let me take my time. He simply and gently brought me to the realization that we were happy together."

— NATHALIE S.

We are the authors of our own lives. By accepting situations and problems as something we are responsible for, we affirm that we are in control of our own lives and our own destinies. Being responsible does not mean that we must bear the burden of the incompetence or the irresponsibility of others. Being responsible means realizing that we are the source of every single event in our lives. We are also the architects of our emotional lives and our relationships. We decide whether or not to invest in a relationship. We choose whether or not to communicate.

Today, I see that I am the source of my relationship and that I can determine what relationship I will experience.

March 8

Making Amends

"If I have harmed anyone in the past (regardless of how justifiable I may think my acts were), I must be disinterested as I admit my wrong and I must make amends and/or whenever I can, reimburse any material damage I've caused. The sooner I can do so sincerely and honestly, the sooner I will be free of the increasing guilt that I have been carrying around unconsciously for all these years."

— Anonymous

It is very hard to live in this world without making mistakes, without harming others, without abandoning our own principles. But when we set out to do good and when we are able to recognize our mistakes, we can mend our ways and live a positive and guilt-free life.

Today, I agree to make amends when I make a mistake. I can examine my conscience and I can admit my mistakes.

March 9

Love Can Be Cruel

Our society has a naively sentimental view of love. We are told that love solves all problems and that if we love enough, we can overcome all obstacles. But love must not be blind. When we truly love, we can do good things and at times, we can set aside our emotions for the greater good of our relationship. When the person we love is harming herself or is on a path of destruction, we can love with strength and detachment without being trapped by the situation. Love is a combination of beautiful sentiments such as tenderness and affinity, but it is also the detachment and power of our convictions within our relationship.

Today, I love with wisdom and strength. I refuse to give in to the tumult of emotions that make me a victim of love. I listen, I look, I am keenly aware of the truth and I am fully prepared to respect my commitments and to shoulder my responsibilities.

March 10

The Ultimate Bond

We are here on earth to love and to learn. To fulfill our earthly destiny, we must communicate with others. The richest, most lasting and most generous form of communication is communication within a couple. I am on earth for such a brief time. I cannot let my life slip away without accomplishing my mission. My partner is another spiritual being with his or her own mission, someone extending a hand and inviting me to share a life path for at least part of the way. How can I refuse to help a being so much like myself and how can I refuse to be helped?

Today, I know that together, we can accomplish our celestial mission by travelling part of our earthly path hand in hand.

March 11

The Vast Reality of Love

"With him, I have a deep sense of fulfilling my mission of love. I love him with my whole being. I would rather die than see him suffer."

— Karen R.

There is a problem in the fact that we use the word "love" to describe a wide range of feelings such as romantic love, affection, family commitment, etc. Of course, all of these are indeed manifestations of love. But love is a much more vast reality, something that approaches divinity. When we choose to give our all to love, we put ourselves in the hand of a superior force. This force, this power of love, is the profound manifestation and the essence of spirituality.

Today, I see that when I choose love, I am in harmony with my true being and I find total serenity.

MARCH 12

Letting Others Love Us

"By asking someone else to give you what you need, you reveal your frailty as a human being and you invite the person you love to share his or her frailty. The reaction to an expressed desire not only brings to the person who needs help the pleasure of seeing a need filled, it also brings to the person who fills the need a feeling of effectiveness and a sense of being capable of giving happiness to someone else. In such moments, each of you has the opportunity of sharing your love and your humanity."

— DAPHNE ROSE KINGMA

Vulnerability hasn't always been viewed as a desirable quality. We know that when we are vulnerable, we may be hurt. We expose our limitations and our weaknesses and we may fall victim to the other person's actions. So many of us have learned not to be vulnerable. There is another side to vulnerability: the ability to ask for help and love and the potential to receive both. In this sense, vulnerability is an openness and a receptiveness.

Today, I prepare my heart to give and to receive love.

March 13

How Can You Mend a Broken Heart?

Very few people have never experienced at least one breakup in a love relationship. These painful events have a lasting effect on us. We can cling to the pain for months and at times, for years. And when, at last, our heart begins to unclench, we love timidly, for fear of reviving the deep hurt. We realize that a breakup is a lot like the sorrow caused by the death of a close relative or a spouse. A breakup awakens in us feelings of failure, abandon, loss, anger and denial that can be very overwhelming. The pain runs even deeper when we have been rejected by a partner. Loss of self-esteem can lead to emotions and feelings that are even more devastating.

But a broken heart can be healed through a new relationship, a resumption of the old relationship, time, therapy, crying, or tranquilizers. All of these remedies have no truly beneficial effect, although they may relieve the pain and fill a void for a certain time. The only cure for a broken heart is to grow, to change, to look straight ahead and to move forward with resolve. We must set aside the illusions we have when it comes to love relationships and we must accept the fact that everything changes and we are responsible for our own happiness.

Today, I know that happiness is accessible to everyone. I know that I can be happy too.

March 14

Sexuality

Sexuality leads to tremendous confusion and difficulty in the human being. The spiritual being has no sexuality of it own; it can only experience sexuality from an outside source. But the body is driven by needs and urges that the human being must understand and accept. Some behavior patterns and perceptions contribute to the growth and development of the individual and others contribute to degeneration and confusion. When we listen to ourselves, we can act wisely.

Today, I know that sexuality belongs within a couple. I can experience a healthy and nurturing sexuality within a loving and committed relationship. Outside the context of a couple, sex becomes a form of slavery. I refuse to agree that it is normal and acceptable to view pornography and sexual degradation on just about every street corner. When I attach too much importance to sex and sexual relations, I stop my own personal development.

Today, I listen to my inner wisdom.

March 15

Yours Forever

So many people are afraid to love. So many people are afraid to be alone, to be abandoned, to be unloved. Deep inside they feel that they have to manipulate, seduce or threaten to keep the people they love close to them. Their fear leads them to take action to protect what they have. Unfortunately, it is true that the love we have in our lives can disappear. Yes, we can be rejected and we can lose a partner. But in love, there is victory. No one can take away the love we have given someone else, the love we have felt. Our loved ones stay alive forever in our hearts and in our life experiences.

Today, I know that love lives on in my heart.

March 16

The Power of a Smile

"I tried an experiment: one day I smiled at every single person I happened to meet along my way. To my great surprise, they all smiled back at me. I didn't quite understand. I tried to find reasons why strangers would react to something as intimate as a smile. And I think I've found the answer: human beings want to establish ties with others and their hearts are wide open to any manifestation of kindness and openness in others."

— Louise H.

A smile is an extremely powerful communications tool. It signals our good intentions and our desire to communicate. A sincere smile is a hand reaching out, a bridge that other people can cross to reach us.

Today, I recognize the power of a smile and I smile to break through isolation and to create new ties of friendship and compassion.

March 17

Being a Role Model

"You must be the change you want to see in the world."

— Mahatma Gandhi

We sometimes forget that we are all role models. The people around us look at us and can find a form of inspiration in the way we behave and in the choices we make. We influence others. Our attitudes and our behaviors influence the people around us. In the same way, we serve as a role model for our partners and for all those we love. If we want to live in harmony and serenity, if we want to be good role models, we must include our values in our day-to-day attitudes and our behaviors. If we want to experience a dynamic and exciting love relationship, we must take a dynamic and exciting approach to life.

Today, I know that I am a role model for my partner. I want to begin building the relationship I want by applying the principles and values that will guide us to the ideal scenario.

March 18

The Trap

"When Anthony hired me as an assistant, I was 21. I knew that he was attracted to me, but he was married and I thought that the attraction would not be a problem. He was a fantastic boss. We often laughed together and he gave me a lot of leeway. I soon realized that he wanted me and that I wanted him. Working together day after day, we had begun to fall in love with each other. We began to see each other outside the office. I knew that it was dangerous, but I couldn't help myself. I was madly in love with him and he promised me that he would end his marriage to be with me, that he was waiting for the right time to tell his wife and to begin divorce proceedings. Our affair went on for two years. When I became pregnant with his child, I begged him to leave his wife and to make a commitment to me. But he didn't see things as that simple. He had realized that if he left his wife, he would lose his business and most of his assets and he would have to pay support. I decided to keep the baby, but I quit my job. Today, I have a new life with another man, but I could have avoided a great deal of pain if I had only stayed away from a man I knew was somebody else's husband."

— Mary S.

Today, I know that my past mistakes are behind me. I can forgive myself, I can live in the present moment and I can look to the future.

MARCH 19

Asking for Forgiveness

"Denying responsibility when we have harmed someone can only lead to more guilt. The best way to find relief is to admit to the error of our ways, ask for forgiveness and repair any damage caused."

— SHARON WEGSCHEIDER-CRUSE

We may believe that there is no need to apologize to a partner or to repair the damage we may have caused them. We may believe that love forgives all or that the other person will accept us as we are, even when we make mistakes. However, of all relationships, our love relationship and our partner deserves the highest respect. Our partner is our most precious ally, our very best friend. Hurting a partner is hurting myself and our relationship. In the most important relationship in my life, it is all the more important to ask for forgiveness.

Today, I know that I am wonderful, but I am human. By accepting responsibility for my mistakes and if necessary, by asking for forgiveness for the harm and the hurt I've caused, I stay on the road to personal development and I keep that road free of obstacles and free of guilt.

MARCH 20

Taking the Time to Love

"I spend a great deal of time with my wife. I love being with her. She is my best friend. When we're together, I feel good and I know that she is happy. We can spend days, weeks and months together — morning, noon and night. We never get tired of being together. I feel that every minute is precious. If I could choose, I'd choose to be with Carol. We're on the same wavelength. We communicate telepathically. I sometimes feel that we're only one person. At the same time, though, I'm a very active person, I have a strong personality and I don't need someone else to make me feel good."

— MARK A.

Today, I invest my time in my relationship. I focus my efforts on communicating with my partner in all the many ways I can.

The Pleasures of the Soul

"I take the time to discover the simple pleasures of life with my partner. I call these day-to-day pleasures "the pleasures of the soul" because they are activities that nurture my being and that give me a love for life. "The pleasures of the soul" include looking at a sunset with someone else, sharing a delicious meal or working in the garden together. We can stroll in the park, go to a movie or listen to classical music. These simple pleasures bring us together and help us discover all the harmony of life as a couple."

— ERIC T.

We are responsible for our day-to-day happiness. We can take the time to enjoy life and to nurture our relationship.

Today, I take the time to stop and smell the roses, listen to the birds sing and look at children playing — life brings me so many small and simple pleasures to enjoy.

MARCH 22

It's Never Too Late to Love

"I'm a bit embarrassed to admit that I was still living with my parents at the age of 34. I had given up on the idea of a love relationship. All of my brothers and sisters were married and I was convinced that I would be the single sibling who took care of our parents. I hadn't been involved with anyone special for a number of years. I spent my evenings reading and I took care of my parents. One fine day, I met John, who was beginning a new job where I worked. He was friendly, kind and uncomplicated. I soon realized that I was looking forward to getting to work each morning so that I could see him again. John was divorced and had custody of his two children. When we began to date, many people told me that I should be careful, he was probably only looking for a mother for his children. But I felt that he was a good man and that his interest in me was sincere. Despite my many years of mistrust and withdrawal, I fell in love with him. He was the best thing that could have happened to me. Now I know that it's never too late to find love in your life."

— BERNADETTE F.

Today, I understand that love is not something you can rush. It takes root slowly and it grows steadily.

March 23

Protecting Our Children

"As parents, we want to protect our children against all possible suffering and against all of life's injustices. Of course this is impossible. But what we can do is create a climate where children are physically, emotionally and spiritually safe. And we will succeed all the better in protecting them if we think that all the children of the world are our responsibility."

— Judy Ford

All children need to know that they are safe and loved. It isn't easy being a child. Their small size and their limitations make them more dependent and more vulnerable. We must all take part in creating a climate of safety and love for the children of this world.

Today, I accept my responsibility for my own children and every other child in the world.

March 24

True Love

"True love is much more than a feeling, a sensation, much more than a magical interlude of emotional inebriation that overwhelms us and stays with us until the full moon has faded to a tiny sliver. Love is a range of behaviors, attitudes, and abilities whose practice creates and maintains a state that we call love. It is a dimension in the form of a relationship that satisfies, vivifies and heals, but it is also the product of a complex effort. In truth, love is "the labor of love" that is apparent only when we realize that in addition to being a gift, it is a very challenging undertaking!"

— Daphne Rose Kingma

Today, I am aware of the "labor of love" that I must accomplish in this world.

MARCH 25

Dependency and Relationships

"Early in our relationship, we had a lot of fun. George liked to go out and have a drink and I liked to go with him. We were young and full of life, we were impulsive. I thought that I'd found the guy I was looking for. George was friendly, funny and a wonderful dancer. My girlfriends envied the fact that I'd found someone so handsome and charming. I was proud of myself. But soon after our marriage, I realized that he liked to drink. I wasn't bothered because he drank alcohol, the problem was that almost every time he went out, he drank until he was dead drunk. I married an alcoholic and I suffered a great deal because of this man's illness. I can't count how many times he would humiliate me in public when he'd lose control, how many temper tantrums I endured, how many lies I swallowed to avoid trouble. As many people know, alcohol and relationships are not a good mix."

— JULIE B.

Drugs, alcohol and gambling wreak havoc in our society. People struggling with dependencies are unable to build a well-balanced and normal relationship. A love relationship requires consistent and hard work. How can someone work at a relationship while they also struggle with a dependency?

Today, I am aware and I refuse to adopt behaviors and attitudes that will lead to a dependency.

March 26

Love Letters

"I like to get love letters from my husband. It's funny, we've been together for almost 40 years, we see each other every single day, and he still sends me love letters. He writes poems for me and he tells me that I'm the most beautiful rose in the garden. He knows that I'm still in love with him, maybe because he still loves me and he acts like a young lover even though he's almost 60! When I get one of his letters in the mail, I play a little game. I tell him that I've just gotten a love letter on scented stationery. "Not another dirty letter from your lover," he answers and laughs. And when I read it, his words bring me back to the day we met and how we fell in love. I love my "old" husband because he's young at heart."

— Anna C.

A love letter takes only a few minutes to write, but it brings hour upon hour of pleasure to the person who receives it.

Today, I take a few minutes to write a love letter to my partner.

March 27

Being Nice at Home

"At times I think that my wife has a split personality. She's friendly and nice with the neighbors, her colleagues at work, the butcher, and strangers, but when she comes home, she turns into a different person. I've seen her yelling and shouting at me and the kids, then turning around and answering the phone in a perfectly charming voice. I told her that we should reverse her roles: why not scream at the office and be nice at home."

— Peter L.

While it is important to be likeable and courteous in our contact with others, it is equally important to create a positive atmosphere within our relationship. We feel that at home, we can be ourselves, we don't need the facade that society demands of us. This principle can be taken to the extreme when we say anything that goes through our minds or when we feel that we can shout just because we're at home. Men are particularly prone to this type of behavior at home. They are kings of the castle and they say what they want to, in any tone at all. When you live with this kind of person, the right tactic is reacting and setting limits — otherwise, daily life is virtually unbearable.

Today, I see that courtesy begins at home. My relationship cannot survive anger and arguments, so I behave accordingly and I create a climate of harmony in our home.

March 28

Feeling Alone

"A long time ago, I abandoned the idea that I can find a decent love relationship. I'm 42 and I haven't been involved with anyone for more than 10 years. When I look in the mirror, as the months and years go by I'm starting to see a friendly grandmother. I have my job, although I would have traded it in any day in exchange for a relationship. I hate to face facts, but men just don't fall in love with me. I'm the kind of person who spends weekends alone waiting for the phone to ring, but it never does. I'm the kind of person no one ever wants to dance with at parties. I'd like to say something to everyone who has experienced a breakup: Don't cry. At least you've been loved by somebody at one point and someone else will probably come along. You'll never know what it's like to be lonely, to feel the anxiety of not being wanted. My life is a nightmare every day. I know what loneliness feels like. Until I turned 40, I used to make an effort, I tried to attract attention and to make myself desirable. But for the past two years, I don't care anymore. I've given up. I know that I'll die alone and unwanted."

— Joan B.

Today, I no longer believe that anyone should ever give up on love. After all, don't they say: "Good things come to those who wait."

March 29

Stop Shouting

"Stop shouting! Shouting at your children or your spouse creates tension and bad vibrations in your home and within your own head. Shouting is never a good idea. Nor is preaching, scolding, lecturing or pontificating. Stop repeating the same things and blaming people. Stop criticizing, directly or indirectly. Stop scolding, stop threatening, stop shouting, stop insulting. For some of us, this is easier said than done. We have grown up in families that shout and scream, where people lay blame, where they mock each other — where all of this seems like normal behavior."

— Judy Ford

Very little can be accomplished by getting angry, by shouting or by using an aggressive approach. Aggression may have the immediate effect of relief, because it lets us vent our anger — but the effect is almost always negative. Gentleness, listening and humor are crucial to good communication and exchange.

Today, I know that I can earn the support and cooperation of my partner by being kind and understanding.

March 30

The Responsibility of Love

Love implies a major responsibility. When we love someone, we let them into the sphere of our intimacy. In return, we ask them to be open to us. We respect, protect and support each other. We respect the other's individuality and needs and we seek their respect and attentiveness in return. Through our own openness, we encourage our partner to love us. Love and friendship implies a major responsibility towards ourselves and towards the other person. This responsibility may be hard to shoulder at time, but is the very source of commitment and belonging.

When love and friendship enter our lives, our entire world changes. Because of our closeness and our influences on each other, we can help or harm, strengthen or hurt, free or dominate.

Today, I understand that love implies a major responsibility and I seek to strengthen the ties of love and friendship in my life in a conscious and responsible manner.

Setting Out to Explore

"I don't know what came over me when I met Diane. Before our relationship began, I used to go out, I used to do lots of different things, I had a lot of friends. But after a few years together, I realized that I never went out anymore. I had no more contact with my friends, I had no more interests except for fiddling around in my basement workshop, looking at TV and mowing the lawn on Saturdays. I think I let myself sink into the comfort and security of living as part of a couple. I felt that all my needs were filled and after the work day, all I wanted to do was go home and rest."

— Michael C.

The couple can easily become somewhere to escape from the rest of the world. The couple is somewhere we feel completely relaxed and safe. But the warmth and security of a couple can be a betrayal in the end. All individuals need self-fulfillment. All individuals need to get out of the home to discover the world and to discover themselves. Without stimulation or challenge, individuals and couples tend to atrophy and to lose their original importance. We should enjoy the warmth and security of the couple by considering it as a base from which we can take on the many challenges of life.

Today, I no longer see my relationship as a place of refuge. I use it as a springboard to the future.

April 1

Appreciation

Sooner or later, everyone needs some form of positive reinforcement. None of us reacts well to punishment or threats. If we want to build a lasting relationship based on love and mutual respect, we must learn to recognize the other person's worth. Each person has an intrinsic value. Each person seeks to make a positive contribution to his or her environment. If we want to foster constructive attitudes and behaviors, we must remember to say thank-you and to show our appreciation to each other. Unfortunately, partners in a love relationship often take each other for granted and they forget that simply saying thank-you can make a big difference in someone's day.

Today, I know that by saying "thank-you" and by recognizing my partner's contribution, I contribute to the vitality and growth of our relationship.

APRIL 2

Commitment

"He refuses to make a commitment. Each time I bring up the topic of marriage, he says that he isn't ready and he tells me that he doesn't like being pressured. He claims that he doesn't want to compromise what we already have for the sake of an outdated religious ceremony."

— CHRISTINE V.

In a couple, the ideal would be to clearly state our intentions and then to take action to make them take form in our lives. Unfortunately, many people have preconceived or false ideas on commitment and marriage. They believe that once they make a commitment, they will not longer be free and they will feel trapped with the same person for an entire lifetime. This notion is completely false. When we make a genuine commitment to a relationship, we find true freedom — freedom to live with a sense of security, freedom from the thoughts and attitudes that harm us as a couple, freedom to build one day at a time.

When we are confronted with someone who refuses to make a commitment, we must determine if the lack of commitment is the result of false notions that can be clarified, or of an unwillingness to go any further.

Today, I am committed to my relationship. Without true commitment, a relationship cannot grow.

April 3

Team Work

"I see our relationship as a team effort. We work together to reach common goals. Each of us has a particular role and particular functions within the team. My work is as crucial and as important as my partner's work. We work together, therefore we are in constant communication and our relationship is a type of cooperative symbiosis. Team work leads us to better results than individual work could. There is more power and more energy in a team and in a single individual."

— Thomas W.

Today, my partner and I work as a team. I know that by working together, we can overcome all the obstacles we may encounter and we can achieve all of our goals.

In-Laws

"My childhood wasn't easy. My parents separated when I was six years old and I never had a regular family life. As a young child and a teenager, I spent most of my time in boarding school. I always felt that there was something missing in my life, until I met Stephany. My relationship with her gave me the family I've always wanted. Her family welcomed me as if I had always been one of them. Her parents love me like a son. Her brothers consider me to be their own brother. I don't feel alone any more. I feel as if I am part of a big, happy family."

— ANDREW P.

Today, I understand the importance of family ties. I want to be part of something bigger. I want to take my place alongside others. I want to feel the sense of belonging a family brings.

April 5

The Power of Love

"One day, when we have tamed the wind, the oceans, the tides and gravity, we should explore the energy of love. Then, for the second time in the history of the world, Man will have discovered fire."

— Teilhard de Chardin

Love is not a feeling as such, although we may feel tenderness and an affinity towards another person. Love is something else. Love stems from our own will to love, from a fundamental choice that defines our relationship with human beings and with life. Love is the frame of mind that results from making life choices. I choose love. I choose to be a loving person. And by choosing love, I transform my life, I transform the way I see the world, I transform my every action.

My love for my partner strengthens our union. I know that I choose to love, I choose to be in our relationship, I choose to be positive. I make these choices every day. I am involved in this relationship by choice and not because of circumstances or chance. I choose to be in this relationship because I love my partner, I love our life together and my choice helps me love and respect myself.

Today, I choose love. I see that I can be an instrument of love within our relationship.

APRIL 6

Growing Old Together

"I'll be turning 40 in a few weeks. People say that 40 is a major turning point. For the first time, we realize that we are beginning to grow old. Youth is a thing of the past. For me, turning 40 is something to worry about. I've accomplished what I wanted to accomplish on the professional level. I love the job I have. Better still, I'm in love with my wife. I know that she loves me and accepts me unconditionally. I'm happy to grow old because I can grow old with her."

— SERGEI M.

Today, I know that I will always be young enough to love.

APRIL 7

Sensuality

"Sensuality gives a physical form of expression to our emotions. The body knows, it urges and it teaches in an eloquent and direct manner. When we are both affected in the same way, when physical love gracefully transports us to ecstacy, we are moved without the need for words to joining of body and spirit, a joining that soothes all hurts and all wounds."

— DAPHNE ROSE KINGMA

Sensuality, touching and physical love belong in a relationship because they are tangible manifestations of a couple's desire for union. Physical love is a captivating activity. Only in a relationship can we make constructive use of the spellbinding forces of physical love. Physical love brings us families and the desire to be together. Some will say that sex and sensuality belong to everyone, to every human context. Therein lies the problem! When physical love loses it real reason for existing, it finds its manifestation in a multitude of perverted and negative forms. Sexuality outside a love relationship leads only to confusion and personal destruction.

Today, I touch my partner with my hands, with my body and with my heart.

Common Chores

"Many men are unaware that life in a couple involves a series of common chores. Housekeeping, socializing the children, cooking and shopping. My husband feels that his chores within the relationship consists of mowing the lawn twice a month and taking out the garbage. I work very hard, but he doesn't seem to realize I do. He seems to think that chores we should be sharing are women's chores. He follows the pattern set in his own family, where his mother used to work like a slave all day and the better part of the evening. But I have a 9 to 5 job and when I get home, I'm tired. He's going to have to change because I can't put up with the situation as it is. I'm exhausted."

— MARY-ANN D.

Today, old stereotypes regarding the couple don't apply anymore. The relationship is a place of negotiation and renegotiation. There was a time when women stayed at home and took care of the children and the housework. Now, to meet the financial needs of the couple and the family, both partners are on the job market. We shouldn't presume that women can do all the work that needs to be done around the home with no help from their partners.

Today, I know that the health and vitality of our relationship depends on a fair sharing of the chores in our home.

April 9

Pleasure

"For a long time I thought that I had to be serious. Even when I was a kid, I didn't have many chances to have fun and to laugh. At a very young age I was given a great deal of responsibility and to me, life seemed serious and even sad. I wondered how other children could be so carefree, how they could laugh and have fun to their heart's content. Now, I know that I can let go, I can enjoy games, I can relax. I learned to have fun when I met John. He embraced life, he enjoyed it and he could have fun under virtually all circumstances. His approach to life was contagious. Today, with him, I can laugh and I can have fun as if I were a child again."

— Robert L.

Today, I enjoy all the experiences life brings me and joy and pleasure are an important part of my life. I look for opportunities to have fun and I share them with other people and my partner.

April 10

For Better and for Worse

Together, we are stronger, more secure, and more able to achieve things. A relationship offers financial security, emotional stability and pleasure. But when our partners fall ill or are in difficulty, our relationship requires that we offer unconditional love, patience and compassion. We are together for better or for worse. We are together in fine weather, when the sun shines, and when dark clouds begin to gather on the horizon. In our relationship, we hope for the "better". However, we know that life is filled with challenges and obstacles to overcome and we must face them with dignity and courage.

Today, I am in our relationship for better and for worse. I have enough love and enough courage to overcome any obstacle.

April 11

Rediscovering Each Other Every Day

"I've been with Linda for several years and I feel that I rediscover her every day. She surprises me, she astonishes me. I look at her and I feel as if I'm seeing her for the very first time. She is so beautiful and so full of energy. I could eat her! Early in our relationship, I was afraid that after a few years I'd get tired of living with the same person all the time. What happened was just the opposite. My love for her gets deeper and deeper. I see her grow along with me and I feel that I am in the company of a sublime and luminous being. I don't know what I could have done in my past lives to deserve her, but I must have done something absolutely wonderful."

— Charles T.

Today, I marvel at the person who shares my life.

Discovering Our Needs

"You have every interest in discovering what your own needs are and finding the words to express them. As you reveal their extent, their nature and as you formulate the deprivations, the losses, the frailty and the talents linked to them, before your eyes you will see emerging an x-ray of yourself. You will see exactly what you are made of, what you really need, and what joy you would feel if your needs were finally met."

— DAPHNE ROSE KINGMA

Today, I take the time to discover my needs and as I discover and identify them, I share them with my partner.

April 13

Admiration

Admiration is a feeling of joy and a form of fulfillment that we experience when we see something or someone that we deem to be beautiful or great. We can develop the ability to admire the person who shares our life. We can cultivate our admiration and we can use it in all our relationships, including our love relationship. Admiration is noble and it lifts us beyond contempt, hatred and conflict.

Today, I cultivate admiration in our relationship.

APRIL 14

When We Were Young

"My life with Celine went by so quickly. It seems that only yesterday we were young, full of enthusiasm and naïve curiosity. I can count on the fingers of one hand the times when we had what I would consider to be real arguments. We were too busy living our life together and making sure our business grew and prospered. I was really lucky to have met a woman like Celine: always in a good mood, hard-working and warm. We're best friends, not only husband and wife. When I was young, I thought that our life together would last forever. Then one day I woke up and I realized I was 60 and our kids had left the home. If we only knew how time slips through our hands as quickly as sand, maybe we'd make wiser choices when we're young. For my part, I'd gladly start my life with Celine all over again."

— ARMAND A.

Today, I will take the time to enjoy every minute because I know that life is precious.

APRIL 15

Freedom

"I think the main reason why my relationship did not work out is that my ex-husband wanted to control me no matter what. Gary is an extremely possessive and jealous man. I think he was always afraid to lose me and his jealously really bothered me. He always wanted to know every little detail: where I had been and who I had spoken to. He was convinced that every man around us had an eye on me and was just waiting for the chance to make a pass. I felt so trapped that eventually, I did it: I took a lover. I think that deep down, I wanted to put an end to Gary's interrogations and his police investigations. I wanted to be free. Not free to be unfaithful, but free of the doubts Gary always had about me."

— FIONA G.

Trust is a key factor in a relationship. Without trust, a relationship quickly degenerates. When people sense that they are not trusted, they can't feel free to act as they want to act or to be the person they want to be. They feel the doubt and apprehension of their partner and it stifles their freedom of expression. Trust is something earned and deserved. If our behaviors cause doubt and anger, we cannot expect to build a climate of trust in our relationship.

Today, I see that trust is a crucial factor in a harmonious relationship.

April 16

Betrayal

"When my husband told me that he was in love with his secretary, I threw everything I could get my hands on at him. I even broke a plate on his head. I suspected he was being unfaithful to me, and when I was told that he was leaving me for a silly little fool, I felt insulted, humiliated and furious. For years, I had worked like a slave for him and the children and this was my reward. I told him that he would pay. I told my lawyer to milk him for whatever we could get out of him. He begged me to be fair, he begged me not to be vindictive, but I just couldn't help it. After all those years of sacrifice and deprival, I just couldn't let it all go without a fight."

— Francine P.

Today, I understand that the feeling of betrayal can lead to a violent reaction. So when I give my word, I keep it.

The Beauty of Taking a Risk

The relationship is a sacred place. In the intimacy and security of the couple, we can be ourselves at all times and under all circumstances. We are with someone who loves us as we are and who accepts us despite our flaws. The couple is a place where we can speak the truth, expose our fears and express our most cherished dreams. If we cannot be ourselves in a love relationship, where can we withstand the light of day?

Today, I show trust in my partner by showing the real Me. I also see that I have the duty to create a secure climate that encourages my partner to express himself or herself freely at all times.

April 18

The Power of the Couple

"About 10 years ago, I was involved in a serious traffic accident. I woke up in the hospital and I stayed there for nearly four months with broken ribs, a broken collarbone, a fractured pelvis, a perforated lung and a host of minor injuries. The doctors eventually told me that they had almost lost me a few times. I had to undergo several operations to rebuild my jaw and to recover the use of my right arm and my left leg. I was stuck in bed all the time, thinking, wondering if I would ever be able to lead a normal life again or if I would be confined to a wheelchair for the rest of my days. My girlfriend Nancy was by my side at the hospital as often as she could, for as long as she could. When I was released, she helped me recover during my year of convalescence at home. We had been together for only a few months when the accident happened and I was surprised to see that she stayed with me and took care of me as if we had been married for years. It was during my lengthy recovery that I realized what a wonderful person Nancy is."

— Terry M.

It is often in difficult times that we learn who our true friends are, who the people who genuinely care for us are.

Today, I appreciate the beautiful things in life and I take nothing for granted.

April 19

Artisans of Joy

"Children are the artisans of joy. With their miniature bodies, they laugh and run and roll about, they bounce and take off in all directions. They get agitated when you take them into your arms, and they are so full of energy that you spot them as soon as they enter a room. They like touching and tasting everything they come into contact with. And they can look into your eyes with an honesty that is so charming, for a second you'll wonder how to respond. They do so many funny things... Life is full of ridiculous things and children have the gift of seeing them clearly."

— Judy Ford

Children experience life creatively. They haven't learned to be cool and distant. They experience things directly and intensely because they have no preconceived ideas. They find life and every single thing in it absolutely wonderful, absolutely amazing.

Today, I choose to look at the world through the eyes of a child. I have fun playing, touching things with my hands and tasting things on my tongue.

Debts

"The first thing we did after we were married was to buy all of our furniture and appliances on credit. What a monumental mistake! We were young and we wanted to set up an elegant and comfortable home right away, so that we could impress our relatives and friends. We soon found ourselves in an impossible situation. John had to work day and night to pay the bills and I baby-sat during the day to help out. Our lives were structured around the debts we had to pay. John used to get home around midnight and he left again at seven in the morning. The only time I saw him was on Sunday and he was always exhausted. We worked like this for four years and in the end, we realized that we were virtually strangers to each other. When I look back, I see that I should have been satisfied with the second-hand furniture my parents would have given us. If I had been, I could have enjoyed my life with John from the very beginning."

— Helen L.

Today, I am aware of the dangers inherent to debts. I will not compromise the quality of my relationship for the sake of owning nice things.

APRIL 21

Trusting Your Partner

"I married an extremely beautiful woman. I'm not sure what she saw in me. I'm an ordinary guy and I have an ordinary job. When Marilyn agreed to come out to dinner with me, I almost fell over. Every guy in the office wanted Marilyn with her red hair, green eyes, gorgeous figure and warm and attractive personality. We dated for a few months and I could see that other people just couldn't believe their eyes. And what I found even more fascinating was that she fell in love with me even though I hadn't done anything particularly special to win her over. At a point, she told me that she'd like to get married. After the wedding, the trouble began. I could see that Tom, Dick and Harry would have loved to steal her away from me. I felt insecure and I was always afraid that I couldn't make her happy and that I couldn't give her everything she wanted in life. I kept thinking that some fine day a rich and handsome man would come along and she'd leave me for him. But besides being beautiful, Marilyn was very smart. She told me: "Jimmy, you're the love of my life. I chose you because I love you deeply and because you're not like all the other men I've known. You have nothing to worry about, I intend to be faithful to our marriage vows for the rest of my life." I really am a lucky guy!"

— JIMMY W.

Today, I know that life has given me all I need to be happy.

April 22

Doubt

"When I discovered that my husband had had a mistress for years, I felt extremely anxious and extremely relieved at the same time. I was caught up in a wave of overwhelming emotions but I was relieved to learn that my intuition had been reliable for all these years. Despite all the lies and the acting, I had always doubted him."

— Evelyn D.

Doubt can slowly seep into a relationship. One partner can begin to feel that the other is not totally committed or totally faithful. Doubt can spoil and destroy a relationship. Doubt can take many forms: jealousy, worry or anxiety. However, doubt never comes about without being provoked. When we doubt, the reason is that we have seen or felt something in particular. And when doubt occurs in a relationship, it is very difficult to dissipate.

A partner can feed or destroy doubt with his or her attitudes and behaviors. Doubt signals the urgent need to be open to each other and to communicate effectively. We need to put our cards on the table and to speak openly about our worries, watching our partner's every reaction. Dialogue will show us whether our worrying is justified and it will help us face the situation.

Today, I choose to put my cards on the table and I refuse to let doubt enter my relationship.

April 23

The Tyranny of Manipulation

A relationship is something undertaken by two people. It is an undertaking that goes beyond individual realities. Some people are unable to build a relationship because they lack the maturity and wisdom to understand a reality that goes beyond their own individual reality. Within a relationship, such individuals tend to sap the other person's energy, love and well-being. For them, a relationship is a one-way street. They are part of a couple only because they want what the relationship can bring them — they are unable to give in return.

Today, I see that a relationship is a two-way street. I also see that the reality in a couple is different and separate from individual realities.

April 24

Small Pleasures

"I love it when the house is filled with the sweet aroma of cinnamon and ginger. I love making desserts for my children and my husband. Baking is a simple activity that brings the family closer together. Each of them come to the kitchen one by one to lick a spoon or to steal a bite of chocolate. The kitchen is warm and inviting and for a time, I am the center of my family's universe. My husband sneaks up behind me and kisses my neck. I tell him he's lucky to have a wife like me, somebody who's such a wonderful cook and baker. He tells me I'm absolutely right and he gives me a big hug. Our relationship can be hard at times, but on days like this, we forget our worries and we focus our attention on the joy of being together, in our home, in its warmth, on the love we feel. My husband and my children are the small pleasures in my life. I feel grateful to have the opportunity to spoil them now and again."

— Eilleen H.

Today, I want to spoil my partner with the small things that bring the most pleasure.

Expressing Our Needs

"When my wife told me she wanted to go back to work, I disagreed. Maybe I was afraid to lose her. With time, she managed to make me understand that she wanted to take on new challenges. That was five years ago. We're still together and we love each other more than ever before. I see how her work brings her fulfilment, how it fills her need for independence. Her return to work revitalized our relationship."

— HENRY D.

To be successful, a relationship must allow each partner to express themselves and to fill their own needs. A relationship cannot survive if it is based on suppressing the needs of one of the two people involved. My responsibility is calling attention to my needs and allowing my partner to find fulfillment within our relationship.

I see that when I express my needs, my partner usually reacts with tenderness and love. She takes pleasure in helping me fill my needs. And I want to make her feel happy and cherished. She is a marvellous human being who deserves my support and my unconditional love. I know that I can let her grow and I encourage her to explore every possibility that can lead her to fulfillment.

Today, I see that I can express needs and my partner can express needs because our relationship is based on love and mutual respect.

April 26

Friends

"Some men feel that they can lead the bachelor life long after they marry. I married exactly that kind of man, but I managed to show him that he would be happier and more secure if he stayed at home more often. Gordon liked to have fun with his friends. He always had a good excuse to leave me alone at home and to go out with his buddies. In the beginning, I tried to get used to the idea that men had to hang around with men. I tried to convince myself that a wife shouldn't meddle in her husband's business and shouldn't try to control his comings and goings. Since I was giving him an inch, Gordon decided to take a foot. He went out four nights a week, and on weekends, he'd go to someone else's house to watch football, baseball, hockey, anything. Eventually, I told him that he had to choose between a life with the wife he loved, or a life with his friends. I had no intention of spending my life knitting alone at home while he was out having fun with his friends. And I told him I was pregnant and that our child needed a father. When he learned that I was pregnant, he stopped and stared at me, his eyes lit up. Our life hasn't been the same since. Gordon has too much fun being a Dad and taking care of Mommy to want to go out carousing with his friends."

— Melany B.

Today, I see that my relationship is my top priority. I have to take an active part in my relationship and I have to be available if I want my partner to feel happy and satisfied.

April 27

Touching

"I believe that we underestimate the therapeutic value of touch. Frank and I have learned to use touch every day to comfort each other, caress each other and relieve stress. It took me a few years to break the ice with him. He told me he wasn't interested in cuddling and touching brought back all sorts of feelings and memories for him. He preferred to keep touching in the bedroom. But with time, I managed to convince him by looking for the best times to approach him. Eventually, I won him over. Now I can say that I'm gratified because part of our communication is conveyed by touching."

— Mary-Ann S.

Every person needs to be hugged, to have a hand held, to feel a soft caress. Everyone likes to have their back rubbed or to have their legs and feet massaged. Touch reinforces a relationship. Love has its physical manifestations. Touching can be a wonderful part of everyday life.

Today, I see that touching makes the heart tender and receptive. I can touch to comfort, to relieve, to relax and to communicate with my partner.

April 28

Rules

"Recently, I read a book called "The Rules", a practical guide for women who want to find and keep a man in their lives. It explains, what a woman should do to avoid bringing things to a head and chasing away a potential Prince Charming. I thought the book was funny at times, but I disagreed with its fundamental theory. I believe that you should be yourself and you should never be ashamed of your intelligence, your intuition or your intentions. The problem with this kind of recipe for love is that once you've hooked the man of your life, you have to be able to live with him, and vice versa. The only acceptable way to live that I know of is to be yourself, with no pretense and no hidden strategy."

— Veronica O.

Today, I know that my relationship requires only that I be myself.

April 29

Our Responsibility

We should ask ourselves a fundamental question: how far does our responsibility extend? We can readily admit that we are responsible for ourselves. We can also easily admit that we are responsible for our children and our immediate family. We can admit that we are responsible for our jobs and for our personal finances. But beyond these immediate areas, we find it hard to define our level of responsibility. We have the impression that we cannot be responsible for areas that are beyond our direct control.

Love relationships fall into areas that are within our direct control. At all times, we are responsible for our relationships, their growth and their quality. We cannot escape the responsibilities of our love relationships because they belong to us and they are our reflection.

Today, I take on the responsibility of our relationship. My happiness and my partner's happiness depend on my ability to shoulder my responsibilities with in our relationship.

April 30

Taking Time to Live

Feeling good implies that I take the time to live, to breathe, to have fun and to laugh. Each day is filled with opportunities to do exactly that! In our mad race in the modern world, we often neglect to enjoy the small pleasures life brings us. Today, I give myself permission to enjoy each moment of the day and to have fun. I pay attention to the small things that warm the heart and when I do, I am all the happier for it!

Today, I know that to make our relationship happy, I must take the time to live life to the fullest.

Spring Flowers

"I think that when it comes to love, I'm one of the luckiest people on earth. I found someone who truly loves me and who has a special place for me in his heart. I found my Prince Charming. This man dazzles me and still makes me tingle with excitement even after 40 years of marriage. I got married at 16 and I have never looked at another man since. I found complete fulfillment then and I feel the same way now. My love for this man is like a spring flower, alive and resplendent with color. I have no special secret for love or for a marriage that has lasted a lifetime. All I know is that if you let your heart speak and if you listen to it, it will show you the way."

— ANGELICA T.

The heart is always young. Our ability to love and to enjoy intimacy doesn't fade with age. Of course, for people who have experienced painful breakups and who have had to hide their true feelings, love can become a fear of love. When we are faithful to our hearts and when we give ourselves sincerely and tenderly to someone who knows how to appreciate us for who we are, love can be the most beautiful of all gifts.

Today, I know that while our bodies age, our hearts are forever young. I will always have the ability to love and I will always see the magic around me.

May 2

The Secret of a Good Relationship

"I spend a lot of time with my wife because we work together. We have a small high-quality textile manufacturing business in Vermont. As you can imagine, we work long hours and in the current economic climate, things aren't especially easy in our sector of activity. Still, I can say that I would not change my life for all the money in the world. My wife and I work hand in hand to make sure that the company runs smoothly and grows steadily. As professionals, we are in constant contact with each other so that we can offer the best product under the best possible conditions. There is no disagreement between us because we're working towards a common goal. Many of my entrepreneur friends tell me about their relationship problems: constant arguing, divorce, adultery, impotence. The list of relationship problems seems endless. We've never experienced any such problems. We've always know where the other one was, we're on the same wavelength and our sex life is as satisfying as it ever was. I used to wonder how, after 15 years of marriage, our sex life could be as satisfying or even more than it ever was before. I believe the reason is that we have the same goals, the same interests and the same mission: living and working together to succeed."

— Bobby J.

Today, I see that a relationship is something two people nurture. I can share my dreams and my aspirations with my partner. Together we can build a beautiful future.

May 3

Pleasure

Life is played out between pleasure and security. We want to have fun and experience every type of pleasure, but we want to maintain our emotional and mental equilibrium. A relationship can offer us the vital balance between pleasure and security. A relationship lets us experience life's pleasures in a stable and secure context. Within a couple, each partner is a companion on the journey to the pleasures of love, relaxation, and all the good things in life. We share pleasure with our travel companion and together, we build a life that makes each of us feel secure.

Today, I can experience all of life's pleasures with my partner. I am careful to bring pleasure and stability to the life we share.

MAY 4

Goodbye Procrastination!

"I decided to stop waiting around and I went out, bought an engagement ring and proposed to her. I think I spent eight hours at the jeweller's choosing the ring I thought she'd like best of all. Then I spent two whole days thinking about how I could propose and when the perfect time would be. Finally, the big day came. The situation seemed just right and I popped the question. A long moment of silence followed. She said no, the answer was no, she couldn't marry me. She didn't want to marry me because she had other things she wanted to do before settling down and she couldn't go out with me anymore because things between us had become too serious too quickly. Of course, I was shocked at having misjudged the situation and the timing so badly. I thought that I had found the woman of my dreams: beautiful, charming and intelligent. I felt humiliated and rejected. But once a few weeks went by, I could see the good side of the whole experience. I had dared to say that I was ready for a lifetime commitment. I could have spent months with this woman before I realized that she wasn't serious about our relationship. So today, I'm free and I know that I have the courage I need to take on a lifetime commitment."

— SIMON E.

Today, I can see how my dreams will come true. I know that I run the risk of making a few mistakes, but a life without risk is a colorless and odorless life.

MAY 5

Financial Independence

"We were sick of the infernal cycle of debts and work: get up, go to work, go home, go to bed, get up... that's all our life consisted of. Society seems to be structured to keep us trapped, prisoners of our mortgages, our cars and our jobs. It was high time to do something else. So we decided to drop out of the system and go live in the country. We wanted a calmer and more down to earth life and above all, we hoped to be as self-sufficient as we possibly could. John knew a lot about farming because his parents had raised bees to make a living and I decided that I'd learn how to raise snails for the commercial market. I had seen an article on this type of business and I knew it could be very profitable. For two years and a half, we got ready to make our dream come true by paying off our debts, taking courses and looking for the right location in the country. Finally, everything came together and we did it! The first years were very hard from every point of view. Now, five years later, we are self-employed and we live well. We haven't given up the system entirely, but our new life has brought us closer together than we ever could have been."

— MADELEINE G.

Today, I want to live the life I see as ideal. Our relationship will be the basis for building a new life, a life that will resemble us and that will make us resonate.

May 6

Overcoming Our Difficulties

"Most of the difficulties and conflicts between spouses can be resolved with communication. When we speak openly and when we make the other person feel that we want to communicate genuinely, the relationship is bigger than any of the problems we may encounter. Misunderstandings and arguments can't withstand the light of communication. Each time a conflict or an argument occurs, something hasn't been said or something hasn't been understood. So my boyfriend and I made a point of developing the habit of speaking openly. When I don't feel good about something, I tell him. When I have an objection to make or a question to ask, I make it or I ask it. When I have doubts or when I'm worried, I share my feelings. We've focused so hard on communication, that my boyfriend and I have become experts. In my opinion, in a relationship there is nothing — nothing at all — that two partners can't or shouldn't discuss."

— Petra H.

Today, I see that the survival and vitality of our relationship depends on communication. Communication implies that each partner can give and receive.

In the Same Boat

When I agree to a relationship, I agree to the fact that I am in the same boat as my partner. I can't say: I have my life, you have yours. We're part of the same crew now. A relationship is like a boat that brings both of us to the same port, in the same weather. What is mine is yours and what is yours is mine. Your problems are mine and my problems are yours. I cannot leave you alone to confront life's circumstances. I must be part of your pleasures and joys, as you are part of mine.

When two people are on the same boat, both of them experience the same events. When I fail to do my share to make the boat sail smoothly, my fellow crew member has to work twice as hard. If I eat all of the food rations, my partner will go hungry. My actions affect my partner and my partner's actions affect me.

Today, I agree that a relationship is a team effort. By working together and by sharing responsibilities and resources fairly, we can grow and we can reach our destination.

May 8

Reading Between the Lines

"I've learned to pay attention to underlying messages, what I call the "unsaid" between us. I believe that the unsaid can be as important and as revealing as the things people say out loud. When I see that Rachel is quiet and pensive, I know that something is wrong. I test the ground to find out what the problem is. When she gets mad for little things, I know that I have to do something before the situation deteriorates. We haven't mastered the art of communication yet. So we resort to indirect forms of communication, some of which are unconscious. There are nonverbal messages, of course, but there are also underlying messages that can go unnoticed if we don't listen carefully. I make an effort to listen carefully and I read between the lines. By asking the right questions, I can understand my partner better and better each day."

— Paul G.

Today, I read between the lines. I pay attention to nonverbal messages because they are as important as words. When I listen carefully to my partner, I am receptive to underlying messages and I make our relationship stronger.

Our Desire to Build

How can we build a relationship without communicating? Yes, there is a type of communication in silence and the unsaid. However, a relationship calls for attention and work. If we want to build a strong, deep and fulfilling relationship, we need to communicate effectively.

Communication is more than saying words and expressing thoughts. Communication is a two-way street. I must express myself freely and sincerely and I must enable my partner to do the same. If I refuse to receive or transmit communications effectively, I cannot contribute to building a relationship. To create ties, both partners must be prepared to receive and to send out messages.

Today, I want to build a relationship and therefore I communicate effectively and I am open to my partner's communications.

May 10

Listening with the Heart

"To be truly satisfying, a relationship requires that we listen genuinely to what our partner is saying. We have to show an interest and we have to want to listen to what the other person says. Listening carefully means not giving advice, not discussing, not criticizing and not evaluating. Listen, and give your partner as much time and as much space at it takes for him or her to express what they want to. When our partners know that they can really express themselves and when we listen to them with our hearts, our relationship is transformed, as if by magic. Turn off the small voice you hear within yourself and listen to your partner, for as long as it takes. I follow this process with my girlfriend and I find that each time I listen intently and show her that I want to hear what she has to say, I feel closer to her. Using this approach, we can solve any and all problems and we can make our relationship stronger."

— Andrew P.

Today, I take the time to listen genuinely. I give my partner the opportunity to speak openly and I listen with my heart.

May 11

The Spiritual Aspect of the Couple

Love of beauty is a spiritual value. Happiness stems from a beautiful life, a harmonious life that we create with the agreement and participation of the people we love and respect. Relationships are part of the beauty of life. When we are happy and satisfied together, our relationship becomes something beautiful and resplendent.

Today, I see that life can be a small masterpiece. Our relationship is an integral part of my masterpiece.

May 12

Adapting Our Communications

"When I was young, because of the way my family was, I developed the bad habit of speaking roughly. But with time and experience, I realized that my tone of voice and my tendency to speak loudly could be surprising and even upsetting to the people I loved and cared about. I understood that to communicate effectively, I had to adjust my way of speaking to my audience. Communication is a very personal thing. To reach someone, we need to communicate in a way that will reach them. Some people turn a deaf ear to gentle or friendly words. Others can't stand someone who speaks loudly or bluntly."

— Gary D.

Today, I look, I listen and I adjust my tone of voice so that I can communicate effectively with whoever I want to reach.

May 13

Caresses

"Caresses are good for the body and the soul; they are a vital need that every human being feels. We have a great need to be touched and for our skin — the silky envelope wrapped around our being, miraculously fine as it is — to be caressed and cherished. This is one of the needs common to childhood and adulthood, all the more since as children, most of us have not been sufficiently caressed, kissed, hugged or simply touched affectionately."

— Daphne Rose Kingma

Today, I know that caresses have a therapeutic effect. I take the time to touch my partner and to be touched in turn.

May 14

Mutual Respect

Mutual respect is the essential factor in communication. How can I encourage the people around me to express themselves frankly if I fail to show them respect or if I fail to give them the right to their own opinions? How can we express ourselves freely when faced with someone who does not respect us? Each person has their own life experience, their own vision of things and above all, the fundamental right to be themselves under all circumstances.

Today, I encourage communication by respecting others and by showing my respect for them.

May 15

One Action at a Time

Just as you build a house by laying a foundation, we build our future with one action, one task at a time, one day at a time. Today, I have the opportunity of taking one more step. I keep my goal in mind and I work hard at achieving it. I don't get discouraged because I know that satisfaction comes from a day filled with work well done.

Today, I take pleasure in doing my best no matter what the task at hand may be. I work hard at making our relationship stronger and I know that my partner recognizes and appreciates my hard work.

May 16

A Relationship is an Adventure

"Today, I live life to the fullest: I jump head on into the adventure that is life. I will not hide from risks. For too long my life has been marked by the boredom of routine. Looking for security, I let myself sink into a routine that eventually began to feel like a grave. Today, I want to explore and broaden my horizons on the physical, mental and spiritual levels. I want to feel the euphoria of new experiences."

— Rokelle Lerner

We can create a wonderful life filled with challenge and adventure. There is no need to compromise. We can be happy and we can find fulfillment in all aspects of life. When we approach life as a wonderful adventure, we are open to new things and new experiences. We can use new building blocks to create a whole new life.

Today, I set out on the adventure of our relationship and I know that both of us will find happiness.

May 17

Solving Problems

To succeed, we must face the problems we encounter each day. If we try to avoid or ignore them, sooner or later they will reappear. But if we develop an attitude that lets us look upon problems in much the same way as we look upon a visit from an old friend, we will never feel powerless. A problem can be seen as an obstacle or a barrier, or it can be seen completely differently. It can also be seen as an interesting variation on a familiar game, something that adds interest and excitement to life. We can look upon problems with a positive attitude because they help us go beyond our personal limitations to travel further on life's path and to become even stronger.

Today, I accept the fact that the key to my success lies in my ability to resolve problems. Instead of running away from my problems, I greet them with open arms.

May 18

Building the Future

"You'll never be someone who's spoiled if you do your own ironing."

— Meryl Streep

Work brings us back to what is crucial in life: building. We are responsible for our own lives and our own well-being. We find fulfillment in work. When we work, we become aware of our place in our relationship, in the community and in the world.

Today, my work lets me build something great, something new and something beautiful which contributes to the lives of everyone who shares this planet with me.

May 19

The Courage to Succeed

It takes just as much energy to succeed as it does to handle a failure. There is just as much work and just as much difficulty in success as there is in failure. We must work actively to grow or to stay small. The exact same effort is involved in both, but it is directed differently. When we put no effort or energy into achieving our goals, we spend enormous energy resisting what comes naturally. Human beings naturally strive to achieve and experience success in all of their undertakings. It takes a great deal of effort to stop short of self-fulfillment.

A relationship is an enterprise built by two partners. They work together to ensure that the enterprise is successful. By communicating, by setting common goals, by sharing responsibilities and by valuing each other's cooperation, they make the relationship strong and successful.

Success calls for a certain degree of courage — the courage to live a more exalting life and to go beyond the limits of the known.

Today, I have the courage to move toward my goal and to make every aspect of my life, including our relationship, a success.

May 20

Interpersonal Ethics

"I do not know what fate has in store for you, but of one thing I am sure: the only individuals among you who will experience true happiness are those who will seek and find a way to serve others."

— Albert Schweitzer

Today, I understand that a relationship must be beneficial for both partners. Our happiness together depends on satisfying my own needs as well as those felt by my partner.

The Power of Our Dreams

A couple can form a mental image of the goals both partners want to reach. If two people want to achieve the same objectives, they must have the ability to imagine themselves once they have accomplished what they've set out to do. Such is the power of our dreams! Together, we can create the future. We can build a mental picture of the situation, we can imagine the context we want. Our mental image will be our guide.

If we have no specific objectives, no specific dreams, how can we realize that our relationship is growing? How can we tell if we are on the right road or if we are drifting away from our ultimate goal? What we imagine as a couple will guide our actions.

Today, I know that together, we can make our dreams come true. We can use our imagination to help us and steadily, we can move closer to our most cherished goals.

May 22

A Prayer for Love

"I don't consider myself to be a religious man. I've never spent much time on God and faith. However, I have come to realize that prayer can be beneficial in times of difficulty. I had just ended a tumultuous relationship and I was in a pathetic state. I kept saying to myself: here I am at 35 and I'm incapable of making a relationship last. I felt that every other aspect of my life was going in the right direction, but I couldn't manage to find a relationship that gave me the emotional stability I wanted so badly. I was completely discouraged. I kept looking back at all my breakups and I began to feel more and more anxiety. That's when I decided to pray and to ask God specifically to give me His support and His love. After a few weeks of praying, I felt better already, more serene and more aware of the type of love relationship that would help me grow. I finally met the love of my life. I don't know if God answered my prayers or if prayer simply dissipated my anxiety and clarified my thoughts. The one thing I am sure of is that prayer helped me through a very difficult time."

— Ben L.

Today, I am in contact with the spiritual aspect of my love relationship. I see that my relationship fulfills me on all levels and helps me accomplish my mission to love.

May 23

Compatibility

"I think that compatibility is crucial in a relationship. Compatibility is expressed through temperament, aptitudes, interests and perceptions. I wonder how two people can build a harmonious and lasting relationship if they are truly different and if each partner is unable to fully understand the other's reality. We can see that opposites attract and are intriguing, but the truth is that birds of a feather flock together. My relationship is happy because my girlfriend and I share a wide range of common traits. We like sports. We have the same opinion on a great many issues. We like to travel. We are both creative and a bit rebellious. We like games, movies and pool. We rarely argue because we usually agree on the small and big things in life. I think that our relationship works because we work at it; we are happy together because we are extremely compatible."

— Alan D.

Today, I concentrate on the things that bring us together and I avoid the things that divide us.

May 24

Laughter

"Life can become a very serious matter very quickly. Financial problems, family and professional responsibilities and day-to-day worries are hard to take. We can be overwhelmed by a number of small inconveniences or we can choose to be optimistic and positive. A sense of humor and a few jokes can make a difficult situation that much easier. I see how much laughter brings to my relationship. I'm always ready for a good laugh and I like to make my partner laugh. We take the time to laugh whenever we're together. I often call her in the middle of the day to share something funny. We've developed our ability to see the funny side of every conceivable situation. I believe that laughing together keeps us together and drives away the stress of daily life."

— Mark Andrew P.

Today, I see the lighter side of life. I can laugh and I can see the funny side of things. When I look at most problems we encounter, I see that it's easy to overcome them with a light heart and a willingness to laugh at ourselves and the situation.

May 25

Ruin

"I think that relationships ruined my life. I was married three times. I thought each time was the right time, but after a while I realized that I had chosen a woman who was going to cost me a lot. Women are attracted to me because of what I can buy them and not because of who I am. Each of my relationships brought me a very temporary happiness and very prolonged suffering. Each of my relationships ended in a nightmare and I had to pick up the tab."

— Bill H.

We often find it hard to believe that a relationship can be turbulent. Unconsciously, we can go towards relationships that will inevitably be trouble. We are not always attracted to the people who are best for us; sometimes our choices are the worst. We should be aware of our own vulnerability and our patterns. Above all, we must take responsibility for our choices. We and we alone decide on who will share our lives. We can decide to grow within a positive relationship, just as we can decide to repeat or to refuse to repeat patterns that lead to our destruction.

Today, I understand that I build my own happiness and my own unhappiness. I cannot simply claim to be a victim of a relationship. I must set out to create the type of relationship that is good for me and that will make me happy.

May 26

Serving Our Partners

Love and relationships are two-way roads. Too many women still feel abandoned. They bear the heavy burden of responsibilities at work, at home and in the relationship. Men are content to live on the edges of the family; they see themselves as breadwinners whose role is to leave home in the morning to go to work, returning in the evening for a well-deserved rest. A relationship requires that both partners shoulder their fair share of responsibilities. Partners agree to be part of a relationship so they can serve each other. Partners agree to be part of a relationship so they can support each other in a shared undertaking. If one partner feels crushed by the relationship, resentment will inevitably destroy it.

Today, I see that my relationship requires mutual cooperation. My partner and I are happy to share responsibilities fairly.

May 27

Being Alone in a Relationship

"I was married for 33 years and I always felt alone in my relationship. I think my husband was just somewhere else. He had the impression that our relationship didn't require any kind of investment or effort. There was very little communication between us. We would say a few words to each other, but we never spoke about important things. My husband always seemed to be very happy with the way things were. He lived his life and he never gave a second thought to much. When he got home after work, his dinner was always on the table. He'd eat, read the paper and then move to the living room to smoke and listen to his favorite TV programs. For the first 15 years of our marriage, I thought that things just had to be that way. But gradually, I looked around and I saw couples who enjoyed life, communicated effectively with each other and shared their experiences. For a number of years I tried to get my husband to see that we could live differently. Henry was convinced that roles shouldn't and couldn't change. My interventions served only to make him angry. When Henry died in 1995, I was sad that I hadn't been able to reach him, that we had never been a real couple or real partners in our relationship."

— Beatrice P.

Today, I am present in our relationship and I listen to my partner. Life goes by so quickly. No one can afford the luxury of waiting until tomorrow to live life and relationships to the fullest.

May 28

A Safe Relationship

A love relationship must be safe and it must make both partners feel secure. Every human being needs stability to grow emotionally and spiritually. Without basic stability, individuals live in perpetual doubt and anxiety. We need to know where we are and who we are with and we need to know that our survival is not in constant danger. Unfortunately, many people live in fear and insecurity. They wonder if their relationship will last, if their partner will decide to leave. Some people have a reflex of threatening to leave or threatening to throw our their partner if things aren't going well. Such a spontaneous and ill thought out reflex keeps the other person in a precarious state, with the constant fear of finding themselves alone and helpless. A relationship cannot grow without a stable and unshakeable commitment.

Today, I know that our relationship is our sanctuary.

May 29

Refusing to Lay Blame

We are responsible for our own misfortunes. It is too easy to hold our partner responsible for our ills. At times of misunderstanding or pain, we may think that the other person is responsible for our unhappiness or discontent. The closeness and intimacy of a relationship makes this transfer of responsibility easier. We often hear: "I'm not happy because she doesn't do this, or she didn't do that. I have to suffer the consequences of her actions. I have to try to get her to stop doing this or that. Or at least I have to give her the feeling that she's abandoned me so that she'll feel guilty enough not to repeat that kind of behavior."

This form of transfer of responsibility is unhealthy and leads only to guilt and a breakdown in communication. In reality, we are responsible for the things that happen around us. We are equally responsible for what happens within our relationship. We are together to share our lives and our experiences and to work as a team. We may be unhappy at the turn of events but we are also responsible for our reactions and our choices in relation to these events. Making a partner feel guilty can only weaken our ability to take on life's difficulties and challenges.

Today, I no longer put the blame on others. I see more clearly that I am responsible for the quality of life within our relationship and in my life in general.

Do it Now!

We all know that it's never too late to build a relationship. We also know that with time, it becomes harder to let go of our preferences; adapting is harder and more limiting and we are less willing to compromise. We can go from one relationship to another, giving long lists of reason why none of them worked out. But we always have the choice of taking position and committing ourselves entirely and honestly to a love relationship.

Today, I see that time is going by and now is the time to commit myself entirely and honestly to our relationship. Life is more than an endless string of repetitions. It is my duty to experience all aspects of life to the fullest.

MAY 31

Mental Illness

"When I started to date Lea, I felt that she was not totally stable on the emotional level. But I was very attracted her and I felt that I could live with her mood swings. After a few months of living together, I saw that Lea had a more serious problem of mental imbalance than I previously thought. She was completely obsessive when it came to certain things. For example, she wanted to know where I was every single minute of the day. She was sure that I was intending to be unfaithful sometime between the time I left the house in the morning and the time I got back home in the evening. She was also obsessively clean. The apartment was never clean enough for her. She could smell odors and she could see dust and dirt that I couldn't and she was always in a state of agitation. She could get very angry and violent when I refused to go along with her. I realized that I had begun a relationship with a woman who had a very shaky grip on sanity. Luckily, I saw my friend Mark on a regular basis and he could see that something was drastically wrong. He has always been very respectful of my choices, but this time he almost begged me to leave Lea. I finally listened to his advice and I believe that he saved my life. While I was living with Lea, I lost all direction in life."

— EDWARD R.

Today, I would never agree to share my life with someone who has a negative effect on my mental health.

JUNE 1

True Love

"True love is a blessing from life, something that cannot be secured by effort. It is a gift of the spirit, not the consequence of action. It is not an objective that we can target, it is a treasure entrusted to our care. When love appears spontaneously, make no effort, simply give in to it! When your intimate relationships offer you moments as grandiose as they are unexpected, do not attempt to analyze or repeat them; open your heart and let them enter with a flourish of light."

— DAPHNE ROSE KINGMA

We all know that love is not something that comes into our lives on demand. We can do everything and anything conceivable to find love, but it will not necessarily come to us. Books that give us recipes on how to love and how to find and keep a partner often neglect to mention that there is absolutely nothing we can do to earn love. Love is given freely, or not at all. We cannot force someone to love us. In the same way, in spite of our best efforts, we cannot convince someone not to love us. Love is spontaneous, but we can choose to nurture or destroy it. The choice is always ours!

Today, I am happy to be loved. Although I know that there is nothing I can do to make someone love me, I can enjoy the love that is in my life and I can create the conditions that will make it flourish.

Contributing

"I think my greatest fear is giving all I possibly can and then being left high and dry by my partner. I think that's why I have a hard time really investing in a love relationship."

— CRYSTAL R.

Equilibrium is vital to any type of relationship. When one partner contributes more than the other, it will be difficult for their relationship to survive. In addition to giving, I must be willing to receive. I am keenly aware of how we share within our relationship because I know that inequalities will inevitably lead to disappointment and failure. I cannot buy my partner's respect and love. Instead, I must insist on fair sharing in all aspects of our relationship.

Today, I understand that a relationship is a matter of giving and taking. If we give too much and receive little in return, we will feel exploited. If we take too much and give little in return, we will feel empty and alone. So I seek equilibrium in all the exchanges that our relationship brings.

June 3

Friendship

"My wife is my best friend. I think that our relationship works well precisely because we've always been such good friends. I say this because I think that when two people are friends, they respect each other. They are interested in each other's happiness and well-being. Two friends know how to have fun together, but they respect the individuality and the rights of the other person. True friends know that they will always be friends and that they can always resolve differences of opinion or conflicts. Good friends never threaten each other and usually, they never really argue. Should a misunderstanding occur, they can discuss matters calmly and each knows that the other will understand their point of view. Good friends can be free and they let others express their true feelings. Good friends like to be together, but they are not dependent on one another. I love my wife tenderly and passionately. I love her because we have been able to build a lasting friendship. I am happy and content in the relationship we have built together. I know who she truly is and I can trust her. My wife will always be my best friend."

— Tony C.

Today, I see that friendship plays an important part in our relationship. I can decide that my partner is my best friend.

June 4

The Power of Truth

"... as long as there is a distinction between what should be and what is, conflicts will occur systematically, and all sources of conflict are a waste of energy."

— Krishanamurti

There is one sure value in this universe: the power of truth. Truth constantly strives to manifest itself because in and of itself, it is the highest manifestation of consciousness and spirituality. But here on earth, truth can be hard to find. We must be extremely determined and vigilant to see truth in things and events. It is as if the universe that we share was based on an enormous lie and through its courage, its work and its intelligence, our spirit must find the path to truth.

There is a fundamental truth in a love relationship: no man is an island. When we invest body and soul in a relationship and when we decide to make it a permanent undertaking, we take up a firm position in space. When we share our life with someone else, we open our heart to a reality that is greater than individuality.

Today, I move closer to the truth and further from lies. When I look at things as they truly are, I can make enlightened decisions. But when I refuse to see the truth, I expose myself to doubt and failure.

JUNE 5

Moving on

"When I told Bernard it was over between us, he didn't want to believe me. He was convinced that he could win me back. All he had to do was to make a special effort and I would forgive him and trust him again. In my eyes, the relationship was over for good. I could no longer love this man no matter how much good will he tried to show. Something inside me had changed. There was no more physical or emotional attraction between us. Bernard did everything he could to make me change my mind. He cried and begged me to give him another chance. I couldn't, it was impossible. The relationship didn't even exist anymore as far as I was concerned. I couldn't turn back the hands of time."

— SALLY E.

Instinctively, we know the moment a relationship is over. But it's never easy to put an end to a love relationship, especially when one of the partners refuses to see that it's over. The sum of the conflicts and suffering we have experienced isn't what makes us aware that a relationship has ended. Unfaithfulness, violence, guilt or lies won't make us understand that the relationship can't go on. Instead, one of the partners must decided that this is the end. And when the decision is taken and is irrevocable, the relationship stops.

If, deep inside, I am aware that our relationship has ended, I must accept the fact and I must look at the future from a new standpoint.

Waiting

"I looked for the ideal woman for a very long time. I was driven by the idea that my life would change and I would be happy at last if I could meet the love of my life. I wasn't happy in the relationship I had at the time because I thought that my partner wasn't really the woman for me. I was caught in an endless cycle of relationships that always ended in failure. Disillusion and obsession were ruining my life. One day, I stopped my quest for the ideal woman and I decided to live for the present. I wasn't in a relationship when I made the decision, but already my life was much more serene. When I met Matty, I knew that she didn't really match the image I had of the ideal woman. But I still enjoyed being with her. After a while, I realized that I had indeed met my ideal woman. I had to stop searching, to find her."

— TOM R.

When we look for something desperately without understanding its true nature, we tend to chase that very thing away from us. Instead of trying to force things, we should be receptive and wait for the right moment.

Today, I keep a distance and I wait patiently for what I want to come to me.

June 7

The Box

"These days, society encourages us to look at marriage like a box. First we have to choose a partner, then we both get into a box. Once we're comfortable, we take a closer look at the person who is sharing the box with us. If we like what we see, we leave things as they are. If we don't, we get out of the box and start looking for a new partner. In other words, we see marriage as an immutable state and we think that its success and durability rests on a person's ability to find the right partner. Divorce is the solution chosen to end an unhappy marriage, the answer for close to 50 percent of all couples. Then they start all over again, hoping that this time they'll choose the right person."

— Harville Hendrix, Ph.D.

Today, I see our relationship as a process and not a static state of being. I have no need to wait to see if the relationship will be satisfying or frustrating. I contribute to building the relationship that I want.

The Death of the Couple

"If we analyze the situation, we see how modern psychology contributes to the destruction of our society. Already, by analyzing statistics on youth, we can see the result of bringing psychologists into our schools. Some people refer to the breakdown of the traditional family unit as the cause of many serious problems, but here again, by advocating attitudes of extreme individuality and sexual promiscuity, modern psychology has pushed us toward total ruin. The strategy of psychologists and psychiatrist is very simple: annihilate the spiritual life of individuals and of families by convincing them, and convincing us, that the source of our malaise is psychological or biological."

— LUKE D.

Today, I see that I am a spiritual being and I share my life with another spiritual being. I will not be confused by all the false notions circulating in modern society.

Being Our Own Advisors

Everyone has opinions. These opinions and viewpoints can be very interesting and can convey truths. But each of us must discover our own truths. We must experience life ourselves, examine facts ourselves and lastly, we must draw our own conclusions. Our society of experts, specialists, gurus and shamans has lessened our ability to search for truth on our own. Instead, we tend to rely on the judgements, analyses and theories of experts. But in the end, we know that we must live according to our own principles, our own truths and our own values.

Today, I am interested in the opinions, viewpoints and advise of others, but I know that in the end, I must formulate my own truths.

June 10

Celebrating the Couple

"I always look for opportunities to celebrate our relationship and the fact that we are a couple. I like anniversaries and official celebrations, but I also look for unexpected occasions to tell my husband that I love him. Recently, for example, John went to court to contest a speeding ticket. He won. He was very proud of himself. I told him he was wonderful and I said that with the money we had saved, we should buy him a nice new shirt and go out to dinner. We spent a marvellous evening together celebrating his small victory and our love for one another."

— Maria S.

Today, I celebrate our relationship. I see that this day offers us opportunities to rejoice and to celebrate our life together.

The Couple's Enemies

"I was in a relationship with Bianca for several years. We were happy together, but for a certain period of time, I had to spend a lot of time at work. During that time, Bianca began to get a bit bored. She made friends with a young single woman and she asked me if they could spend time together. I had no objections because I was very busy with work. After a while, all Bianca ever talked about was Linda, her new friend. I could see that her single friend was taking up more and more time and space in Bianca's life. Unfortunately, I didn't react fast enough. With Linda's help, Bianca had begun to create a new identify for herself, outside our relationship. When I saw what was happening, it was too late. Bianca had already moved out and I had no way of reaching her."

— LORENZO L.

A relationship must be solid to withstand outside influences. Both partners must be present and committed to keep enemies from breaking down the relationship. In our professional and social circles, there will always be people who want to break our emotional ties and interfere in our relationships in one way or another.

Today, I am more vigilant than ever before. I want to maintain and strengthen our relationship, so I am sensitive to the outside influences that can harm our life as a couple.

Making Contact

"When Lucy is worried, she tends to keep quiet about it. When I'm concerned over something, I tend to discuss it. Sometimes I verbalize a bit too much and I say things that I regret later on. However, I at least I can get things off my chest and I can say exactly what's bothering me. My challenge within our relationship was expressing my grievances in an acceptable way. I tended to lose control and to go too far in expressing my emotions. With time, I learned to take a step back and to speak objectively about day-to-day problems. Today, I communicate effectively, in a way that encourages listening, and I avoid making Lucy feel that I want to bite her head off. I can see that a calm and open approach gets much better results. For her part, Lucy had a different kind of challenge to handle. She tended to keep everything bottled up inside and she avoided discussing touchy subjects. When she was angry or unhappy, she could spend hours and even days without saying a word. I would suspect that something was wrong, but I couldn't manage to get her to talk about it. Little by little, I got better at decoding her silences and I learned how to get her to speak up."

— MATTHEW G.

Today, I accept the fact that we are different and that we have our own ways of overcoming adversity. But I also believe that by communicating, we can reach each other within our relationship.

June 13

I'm Here for You

"In 1980, I accepted a job in a newly opened office in a suburb and we were forced to move to a small city about 100 miles outside of New York. I couldn't have predicted that the move would change everything for us. We lived in a lovely country home. The children were lost for the first few weeks, but they ended up adapting to the change. However, my wife Sylvia couldn't settle down to our new life. She was used to being close to her job, her friends, her family and her favorite restaurants and boutiques. Now she was 100 miles from her work, her family and the big city. I could see that she had the blues and that depression wasn't far away. I tried every imaginable tactic to make her feel better, but nothing seemed to work. Several times I tried to get my old job back, but the company executives told me that my talents were needed at the new branch. I had to choose between my relationship and my career. I chose my relationship. I left my job, we sold our country home and we went back to New York. Our financial situation was a bit precarious for a few years, but my wife was smiling again. In my eyes, my wife's smile is worth much, much more than a prestigious job."

— Martin J.

Today, I am more interested in the quality of our lives than I am in accumulating material wealth and social prestige.

June 14

Being Yourself

"What I like about Patrick is that I can be myself under any circumstances. I know that he loves me for myself, with all of my qualities and all of my faults. I can make a mistake without being afraid that he will withhold his love or that he will criticize me. I can be beautiful or messy, boring or funny, he takes me as I am. What a comfort! What peace of mind! I know that to grow within our relationship, I have to be myself all the time and under any circumstances. And I have to give my partner the same permission to be himself, express himself freely and live his life as he chooses. I can't tell him what to think or feel. He has his own perceptions and his own reality. Being yourself takes no special effort. Being yourself is being spontaneous, expressing yourself fully, never holding back. By being myself, I am present and I can experience my relationship directly. By being myself and by letting my partner be himself, I feel that I am growing in a relationship that is honest and alive."

— Anna V.

Today, I know that I can be myself with my partner and I give my partner the same opportunity.

June 15

The Magic of Silence

"When I'm with Laura, I feel that we are one and the same person. To some extent, we function through affinity or telepathy. I know what she is thinking and I feel that she is part of my thoughts and part of my emotions. We can spend hours together without saying a word, yet we are in total and perfect communication with each other."

— Claude R.

I've always felt that there is a type of magic in silence. Silence is alive and active. Silence is a space that provides a glimpse of all the possibilities of life, all that is not manifest in the cacophony of day-to-day life. My heart and my soul seek silence to manifest themselves, to speak. In moments of tranquility and silence, I find my calm and my courage and I feel rested. Each day, I seek the refuge of silence.

Silence must have a place in a relationship. When two partners are close, words are not necessary. Communication can be established without conversation.

Today, I cultivate quiet and silence.

JUNE 16

The Love that Transforms

Relationship is a dynamic framework of growth and change, particularly since it calls upon our natural ability to adapt. We should not feel obliged to change and to compromise. Rather, in the interest of the relationship, we make choices that encourage and increase the harmony within our couple. The choices that we make each day, big and small, reinforce the ties between the relationship's partners. Some may say that this perception is idealistic, but look around and you will see that most couples have found a modus vivendi based on mutual adaptation.

Today, I am undergoing change. I see that I am growing and that I am moving closer to happiness.

June 17

Faithfulness

"For a few years, we had an open relationship — we were open to extramarital affairs. We were acting this way with the admitted goal of not ending our relationship by making a formal commitment. After a while, we realized that we were unhappy. Deep inside, I wanted to be with her and her alone and the lack of commitment between us was a heavy burden. When I told her how I felt, I was surprised to hear her admit that she felt exactly the same."

— Steve L.

Today, I see clearly how important faithfulness is in a relationship. Commitment in a relationship is an agreement between two individuals. The agreement should involve no reticence and no secrets. If I break the pact I have made with my partner, I betray my own integrity and I doom my relationship to failure. Today, I believe in faithfulness because I have experienced the disastrous consequence of secret and unfaithfulness. Faithfulness brings stability and harmony between partners. Unfaithfulness has a profoundly destabilizing effect on a relationship. No one can consciously claim that a loved one's wandering leaves them indifferent. Without a framework for moral conduct, a relationship will never last.

Today, I know that faithfulness is a vital factor in a relationship.

The Honeymoon is Never Over

"I like the first six months of a relationship. What I enjoy in a relationship is the honeymoon. You get to know each other, things are lovey-dovey, the sex is great and you only see the good sides of your partner. You feel alive again, full of energy, the world is beautiful. When the first six months are over, I bow out. I don't feel like handling all the problems that come after that: having to account for your comings and goings, seeing passion fade away, seeing life become more boring by the day. I'm there for the fun in a relationship, I don't need the drudgery."

— MALCOLM D.

The honeymoon can last a lifetime. Whether it does or not depends mostly on our attitude to the commitment that a relationship requires. We have to want to experience all the phases of a relationship. The honeymoon is in our heads and in our hearts. Each partner decides to renew his or her love and passion each day. A relationship requires a sustained effort. Each partner has to be as interested in the other's happiness as they are in their own. Individuals who look for pleasure and facility will never experience a true love relationship.

Today, I want to bring passion and intensity to my relationship. I refuse to let my relationship slip into the boredom of a set routine. I want to live each day as if it were the beginning of an exciting new adventure.

June 19

Love in an Extended Family

"When I met Victor, I had lost all hope of building a new life with a man. My first marriage, with a Dutch man, had been painful. I had done all I could to make Gerald happy, but despite my efforts he went back to his country, leaving me behind with two small children. It wasn't easy for me to raise two kids alone with not very much money. Despite feeling rejected and abandoned, despite the loneliness and the financial difficulties, I managed to raise my children in a climate of love and security. I was given very little help from my family and my friends, mainly because they though I was responsible for the breakup. When Victor came into the picture I hardly noticed him at first. He moved into the apartment next door to mine. He looked nice, but he was shy and reserved. He was in the same boat as me: two children to care for and an ex-wife that wasn't too interested in what happened to them. We had known each other for more than a year before romance blossomed between us. We were both afraid. I could see that Victor was a calm and gentle man. He never raised his voice with the children and he gave them a great deal of affection. Gradually, I fell in love with him and we became a couple. He loves me passionately and tenderly. I hadn't realized how much I missed tenderness and romance until I met Victor."

— Belinda V.

Today, I give love a chance. I open my heart to the possibility of discovering love in my life.

Sharing Household Chores

"I was raised to do my share of household chores. My parents taught me that personal discipline, cleanliness and mutual help are vital to the family nucleus. Each of us has small chores to do each day: helping to prepare meals, washing the dishes after meals, taking out the garbage, walking the dog, etc. Today, I see how this discipline helps me in my current relationship. There is a very nice type of cooperation between Lawrence and me. We share the work that has to be done around our home and it doesn't even seem like work to us, it's too much fun!"

— TOM M.

The quality of life in a relationship often manifests itself in small things: sharing a clean and well decorated home, sharing household chores, eating well, sleeping well and having fun doing the small things in life every day. If day-to-day jobs are a burden for one and a non-issue for the other, a relationship will begin to deteriorate very quickly. But if partners are willing and happy to work as a team, life suddenly becomes much easier.

Today, I share in household chores. My partner and I can have fun taking care of our home together. Living in a couple is a lifetime project carried out one day at a time.

Being Faithful to Myself

"Faithfulness is the only currency that keeps its value over time."

— FRANÇOIS GARAGNON

Faithfulness is a very noble value. Being faithful in a love or business relationship proves our maturity and our worth as a friend or associate. When we are faithful and when we show that we deserve to be trusted, we can build solid relationships that can withstand the test of time.

But before being faithful to others, we must be faithful to ourselves, to our values, to our principles and to our own experience of things. Being faithful to ourselves means recognizing our right to choose. It means recognizing and learning from our mistakes and rewarding ourselves for the good things we do. Being faithful to ourselves means listening to ourselves and to our hearts even when our environment encourages us to follow the group trends. It means having the courage of our convictions and the strength to make choices and to accept our individuality.

Today, I know that by being faithful to myself, I respect myself and I give myself every opportunity of being happy within our relationship.

June 22

What Men Like

"Most women know what men like. Men like to be spoiled, they like to be complimented and to be told that they are the handsomest and the strongest of all; they like to be served and they like to see their woman in the kitchen, preparing their favorite dishes; men like to be right even when they pontificate on a topic they know relatively little about; men like to give orders and to see others obey them; men like to make love whenever they want to; men like women who forgive them no matter what, and who give them the freedom they need to do whatever they want. While most women know what men like, women aren't always willing to give it. Why? Because women want the same things."

— Deirdre D.

Today, I will give my love freely and generously to my partner, the most important person in my life.

June 23

A Second Chance

"Martin asked me for a second chance. I couldn't say no, but he had done what I considered to be the unthinkable: he'd slept with my sister. I was extremely upset. I'd lost all confidence in two people I loved deeply, at the same time. I could understand that my sister had flirted with my boyfriend, but that he'd acted on the flirting... Martin swore that it would never happen again and that he'd do all he could to win back my trust. My sister went into hiding. When I confronted her, she told me that I didn't deserve somebody like Martin. According to her, I always got everything I wanted; she was much more approachable than I ever was and she deserved to be happy in a relationship with Martin. So I felt anxious and I was living in an atmosphere that I felt was unacceptable. How many years would it take before the situation got back to normal, if it ever did? What impact would the incident have on our relationship and my family life? I felt betrayed and humiliated. After a few weeks, I decided to end my relationship with Martin once and for all. I think I wanted to start a relationship on a new basis. Getting back together with Martin could have been a good choice, maybe even a better one, but I didn't want any negative vibrations in my living space."

— Catherine S.

Today, I decide what I want and what I don't want. I share my space with those who love and respect me.

June 24

Living Passionately

"Sydney comes back from work and flops down in front of the TV. I like the fact that the man I have around me every day needs almost no maintenance! He's always in a good mood and he assures me that he wouldn't change anything about our life together. Meanwhile I fantasize about passion and adventure and I tell myself: well, maybe in the next life."

— Victoria P.

Where does passion come from? How can we change an ordinary relationship into a passionate day-to-day adventure? The start of any relationship is always a time of passion, but how can we nurture and sustain the initial passion to make it last a lifetime? The question is complex because of the link between security and pleasure, between adventure and danger. A relationship should be fuelled by passion and adventure, but it should not jeopardize the basis that gives each partner a sense of comfort and security. Passion and adventure can be found in the things partners do together. When a couple focuses on an exciting life project, their relationship is revitalized. The new excitement they feel spreads to all aspects of their life together. They both look in the same direction and together, they work towards a common goal.

Today, I see that adventure and passion lie in the ability and willingness to share projects with my partner.

Sexual Fantasies

Some people believe that they have to live out their sexual fantasies. They think of sexuality as a panacea. They believe that suppressing sexual urges can harm an individual by crippling his or her emotional growth. And such urges could be expressed by virtually any type of aberrant behavior. These false concepts come to us mainly from the writings of Freud, Reich and company, and they are founded on the principle that our problems stem from a suppressed infantile sexuality. Unfortunately, these falsehoods have taken on such proportions that many people are convinced that they must imagine and experience all sort of unusual and unconventional sexual experiences.

Luckily, through relationships and the family, two individuals can have sexual relations based on love, tenderness and the strengthening of emotional ties. In a relationship, we can share our desires in total security and we can create a romantic life and a love life that resembles us and that brings us closer. Often, sexuality is less contaminated within a relationship because in this context, it is a healthy and normal expression of the love we feel for our partner.

Today, I see that sexuality belongs within the dynamics of a relationship.

Preconceived Ideas

We often cling to preconceived ideas that hurt our life as a couple and that may even prevent us from building a relationship. These preconceived ideas can result from the analysis of our parents' marriage, from the publications we read, from the advertising we are exposed to or from our education. Preconceived ideas can destroy our ability to live within a relationship because they are fundamentally false concepts that we attempt to apply. For example, we may entertain the idea that a couple should never argue. If arguments do occur, we may believe that our relationship won't last. We may believe that we will never be happy until we meet the person for us. And if we don't meet that person, we will be unable to build a viable relationship. And so we spend a lifetime looking for the person, meanwhile missing out on the opportunity to share our lives with any number of wonderful, enriching candidates.

All of us must do own analysis of the preconceived ideas that limit our ability to live within a happy relationship. Living as part of a couple can by an exciting and exhilarating experience. But first, we must free ourselves of the false principles that prevent us from reaching this particular goal in our lives.

Today, I free myself from preconceived ideas and I seek to live in the present.

The Barriers on the Horizon

A relationship can entail a number of barriers. The latter determine no the quality of our relationship, but our attitude to wards it. Life itself offers us a series of challenges that we must take on if we want to succeed and be happy. The same holds true for relationships. The couple offers an ever-changing and dynamic context that brings us obstacles and barriers that we must overcome if we want to be happy together. Sometimes the barrier to our shared happiness exists within the relationship itself, within our partner or within ourselves. One by one, we must break down these barriers.

A couple may be burdened with financial problems. A perfect example of a barrier we can and must overcome together! A barrier may also exist within the other person and it may take the form of a fear of long-term commitment, difficulty communicating effectively, or the fear of emotional closeness. We can help our partner go beyond his or her personal barriers to living in a relationship. Barriers can also come from within ourselves. We must be vigilant and open if we are to overcome our limitations. Barriers are neither walls nor prisons. They are obstacles on the road to happiness and we decide to overcome or bypass them together.

Today, I know that together, we can overcome any and all obstacles.

Being of Service

"Life teaches us that the only worthwhile endeavor is serving others."

— LEWIS CARROLL

A relationship requires that we serve our partner. Too often in the past, men entertained the false idea that they were the king of the castle and they could expect to be served by their wives. Women eventually refused this type of servitude. Man-woman relationships have changed. Now each is expected to share and participate equally in a relationship. But a couple cannot last if one person refuses to serve the other or if one feels debased when serving a partner. Within a couple there should always be an equilibrium based on equal sharing. Equal sharing presupposes that we offer our time, our work and our love and the other person does the same. Each partner's tasks and activities may and should vary, but within the context of sharing and mutual trust.

Today, I know that I can serve my partner without losing my self-respect or my individuality.

The Battle of the Sexes

A relationship should never be a war zone where each partner seeks to control the other with a show of strength and domination. Violence and emotional warfare cannot serve as a basis for a relationship. I do something you don't like and then you do something I don't like to punish me and to make me pay. A vicious circle of this type can lead only to perpetual conflict and eventual breakup. We build up so much anger and bitterness that it becomes impossible for us to stay together.

How can I put an end to this endless cycle of conflict? The answer is becoming fully aware that I am responsible for my happiness and for my partner's happiness and laying down my arms. When one partner stops the battle, the other inevitably joins the cease-fire as well. The crux is resisting the temptation to go back to old habits. Eventually, with patience, by reestablishing communication and by forgiving, together we can restore harmony to our relationship.

Today, I want to experience peace and harmony in our relationship.

June 30

Despite All the Problems

We know that despite all the problems, conflicts and difficulties it may bring, life in a relationship has many advantages and rewards. Life as a single person can be viable and even enjoyable, but life in a couple offers us all the richness of love and true commitment. Those who are not involved in a love relationship know this instinctively. At times, a single person who has gone through painful relationships may become resigned to a life alone, for fear of being subjected to a rejection and a breakup yet again. A single person may find it difficult to begin a relationship because he or she feels confined to look for a partner under a certain set of circumstances and within a limited number of contexts.

No matter what we may have experienced in the past, love is always possible. The first step to a relationship is made in our heart. The first step is admitting our desire to share our life with someone else; from that moment on, our efforts converge in this direction and suddenly, life becomes a reflection of the harmony of the universe.

Today, I see the advantages in living as part of a couple.

July 1

Opening Your Heart

"Nothing can make you happier or make you feel better about yourself than a true and honest emotional exchange with another human being. Nothing is more wonderful than being able to tell someone else who you are, be able to open your heart, be able to show your true colors, be able to meet another person with the same level of refinement."

— Daphne Rose Kingma

A relationship flourishes only in a climate of security. A climate of security exists only when we can count on our partner. A relationship is secure when we know that our commitment is sufficiently strong to withstand life's tests. In a secure relationship, we can be ourselves and we can communicate freely. The ability to be honest at all times gives us the assurance that we can be ourselves at all times and under all circumstances.

Today, I seek to create a secure climate in our relationship.

The Seasons of Love

"My relationship changed with time. I no longer have the same contact as I used to with my wife. We've been together since 1944. The last 50 years have been filled with changes and our relationship had to keep step or it would never have survived. In the beginning, I had very conventional ideas on the couple and the family. I saw my wife staying at home with the children, and I was the breadwinner. But somewhere along the way, the roles were reversed. After 20 years as a teacher, I had to retire for medical reasons. At the age of 42, I found myself staying at home while my wife went out to work. We've overcome all of the obstacles thrown our way because we decided that we were together for life. I learned to get to know my wife and she knows me better than anyone else in the world. We love each other and we have a deep respect for each other. She is the light of my life."

— MORRIS D.

Each relationship must go through its own seasons. Spring and summer are filled with energy and accomplishment. Fall and winter bring us the calm and security of age and reason. Together, we can go through all of these stages and we can overcome all of the obstacles in our path. I am yours and you are mine.

Today, I am with you and tomorrow, I will be with you. I will cross all of the seasons of our relationship.

JULY 3

Never Go to Bed Angry

"I've learned that we should never go to bed angry. When we go to bed without having settled our differences, our sleep will be disturbed by our state of mind. And when we get up in the morning, we are likely to want to continue the argument or we may simply be in a bad mood. By following the adage: 'Never go to bed angry', we find the discipline to maintain good communications and we find it easier to find the solutions to the problems in our relationship. When we settle arguments before we go to sleep, we can do so in peace and the next day, we get up in a good mood."

— ALEX D.

The ties of communication in a relationship must be maintained and reinforced. Misunderstandings and conflicts are perfectly normal, but we must find mechanisms that enable us to overcome our differences and reestablish proper communications. Most problems related to relationships can be solved fairly easily when we agree to talk things out and to look at things from the other person's point of view. Why stay angry when we can find a quick solution to our problems?

Today, I know that I must always keep the channels of communication open between my partner and myself.

July 4

The Perfect Man

"I spent my adult life looking for the man of my dreams. I focused on the superficial. I evaluated potential candidates on the basis of their physical appearance, their mannerisms, their prestige and their clothes. I couldn't see the man behind the facade. I had a precise image of the relationship I wanted and any man who deviated from my ideal was simply unacceptable. I regret having been fussy and having rejected a great many men without even a second thought. I gave up the charade when a friend told me that the perfect man just doesn't exist. The important thing is to find someone who is compatible, someone I can get along with and someone who is willing to work with me at building a happy relationship."

— Laura P.

The perfect man or woman exists only in our dreams. There's nothing wrong with dreams, but we should dream with open eyes and an open mind. There are certain determinant factors to consider in a relationship: compatibility between the two people it involves, mutual admiration; feeling loved and respected; being capable of solving problems. These factors determine the stability and durability of a relationship.

Today, I keep my eyes and my mind open for someone who wants to build the same type of relationship as I do.

July 5

The Perfect Woman

Our society has deified the female body. If we look around us, very few women correspond to the ideal type presented in magazines, advertising, fashion and the cinema. Many women feel obligated to comply with this prefabricated image. And many men are in search of a woman who exists only in the collective imagination. When we agree to enter into a relationship with a woman, we agree to form a couple with a spiritual being, not a physical body. The physical body is an envelope for the spirit. We do not fall in love with an envelope, although we might be attracted by it. The body changes and ages. The spirit is forever young.

Today, I know that the body changes and grows old. I will invest my love in a spiritual being, not a body.

July 6

Daring to be Spontaneous

"I told him that I was sick of walking on eggs. I couldn't do anything without having to explain and justify myself. When Joe decided to take personal development courses, he changed for the worse. Before, we had the same kinds of problems most couples do. But now, he constantly has to analyze every gesture and every word. I have no desire to be analyzed and censured all the time. I don't care what the high priests of personal development think. I want my old Joe back."

— Sylvia P.-B.

In a relationship, we abandon ourselves to a specific reality. The reality of a relationship is one of co-creation and it requires that each partner be free and express themselves freely. It is wrong to try to analyze and dissect each other's smallest gestures and most casual words; life as part of a couple should be lived one moment at a time, one day at a time, with no need for lengthy analysis. When things don't go as smoothly as they can, we should seek to understand and rectify our behaviors. But when we look outside the relationship or outside our own reality to find answers, we find the answers that belong to others. By working together and by being sensitive to the demands of our own couple, we can always find solutions.

Today, I live my relationship to the fullest. I have no need for constant analysis to participate in my relationship.

JULY 7

The Baby and the Bath Water

When we focus our attention on the negative aspects of our relationship, we may believe that the relationship is hopeless and that it can't possibly last. When we're happy and when we feel good, we're convinced that the relationship will last forever. Our emotions have an effect on our perceptions. When we feel bad, we may believe that our partner is the source of all our unhappiness. When we feel good, we may feel that the other person brings us all the happiness and joy in our life. When conflicts occur in a relationship, we should ask ourselves: How have my feelings influenced my reaction to the situation? Sometimes stepping back can help us see things clearly, as they really are. When we are well rested and in a good mood, we can take on the problems life brings us.

Today, I focus my attention on the positive aspects of my relationship.

July 8

Consolidating Trust

"My relationship with Caroline is based on mutual trust. I'm a sales rep for a large engineering firm. I travel all over the world to negotiate agreements. I'm away from home at least six months a year and I can say in all honesty that I have an excellent relationship. I can say I do because I know that I can trust my wife and I know that she trusts me. It wasn't always the case. We spent a few troubled years when neither of us felt comfortable with the number of trips I had to make and the amount of time we were apart. We talked about the situation often and more importantly, we built a relationship based on trust. Trust is something you earn, of course, and it comes about when both partners show stable and predictable behaviors."

— Frank B.

A relationship based on trust grows stronger with experience. It is something that two people build, by defining together the conditions and behaviors that will maintain and consolidate mutual trust. We quickly see whether or not we can trust someone. Our perceptions are based on our observations and our intuition.

Today, I look for ways to build a relationship based on trust. I am worthy of trust and I can trust my partner.

July 9

Bisexuality

More and more people advocate bisexuality. More and more often, we hear and we read about individuals who have had sexual experiences with both genders and who define themselves as bisexuals. Bisexuality contributes nothing to a love relationship because it introduces a new element that is neither productive nor geared to creating a climate of security. The temptation to try new sexual experiences can be great, but we should be aware that there is a price to pay for this type of activity. The couple is based on a stable relationship between two people of opposite sexes (or of the same sex, in the case of homosexuals) and the relationship enables the two to discover and share their respective identities and intimacies. When we look outside the couple to satisfy our sexual desires, we weaken the ties that keep us together. In the same way, when we introduce a third person into the intimate circle of the couple, we expose our relationship to outside influences that are beyond our total control.

Today, I see that a relationship is an intimate circle that must be protected against the negative influences that can come from the outside.

July 10

Easy Relationships

Sometimes, we think that some relationships are easy, and others are hard. We look outside the couple and we think that some couples have an easy life; they get along wonderfully well and apparently they have no major problems. I believe that some couples manage to establish a modus vivendi, and others don't. Some couples have established the rules of the game and they follow them, and others have failed to set down a stable basis for cooperation. If we have no stable basis for working together, each problematic situation will shatter the relationship's harmony. If we know the rules of the game, we can act freely within the limits that we have set.

Today, I work with my partner to establish a stable basis for mutual help and mutual respect.

Making a Relationship Successful

When we realize that each partner is responsible for the quality of life in a relationship, we stop believing in miracle solutions and magic recipes. A relationship is a dish that always contains a certain number of basic ingredients:

- a deep and unshakable desire to experience in harmony a life based on sharing, communication and mutual respect;
- systematic and continuous work to achieve this objective by eliminating all factors and obstacles that can hinder its achievement;
- the ability to recognize and celebrate each day of life as a couple.

Of course, there are predetermined factors that can help us or hinder us as we work to achieve this objective. But such factors are secondary when the objective is clearly defined and when we begin the process that will lead to its achievement.

Today, I know that I am entirely responsible for the quality of life within my relationship. I am determined to begin the process that will lead us to our objective of a solid and happy relationship.

Building Reserve Funds

Our parents and grandparents understand how important it is to save. They lived through very difficult times when it was often hard to find food and clothing. Their generations were profoundly affected by the hardship and poverty of the Depression and economic recessions. Today, society encourages us to consume today and pay tomorrow. And in the process of accumulating material wealth and amassing personal debts, we forget how important it is to save and to build a reserve fund.

Life in a relationship can be hard if we're unable to put some money aside and if we have no financial reserve. When we're always down to the last penny, unforeseen events can quickly plunge us into a catastrophic situation. By building a reserve fund, we can protect our relationship against financial disasters. If one partner loses a job, we have funds on hand to tide us over. If we want to undertake new projects, the financial resources we need are available.

Today, I understand the importance of managing family finances soundly and of saving for unexpected expenses.

July 13

Making Failures a Positive Experience

"Most of the limits in our lives are those we impose on ourselves. Whenever we are firmly convinced that we can achieve something, generally we do. But conviction is something very different from wishful thinking. Taking your wishes for reality is a passive tactic; conviction and self-affirmation makes us clear a path through life's obstacles or manoeuvre around them to reach our ultimate goal."

— Sue Patton Thoele

A relationship forces us to assess ourselves against an objective reality. We have to look at the consequences of our actions and learn from them. Failure is our environment's objective reaction to our actions. When I fail, I have to determine exactly what actions, what behaviors or what factors have contributed to my failure. Failure can teach me valuable lessons. It is said that human beings learn more form their failures than they do from their successes.

Today, I see that there will always be something new for me to learn. I will use my failures to learn and to grow stronger. I can embrace failure rather than trying to escape it or trying to avoid risk.

July 14

Being Flexible

We sometimes hear that as we grow older, we are more set in our ways. We should decide to be more flexible as we age. A relationship requires extraordinary flexibility. We must adapt by adopting new perceptions and new behaviors. And this cannot be done without making a fundamental compromise. By agreeing to see life from different points of view, by agreeing to borrow our partner's perceptions, we can make enlightened choices. It is impossible to build a happy relationship if we are rigid and uncompromising — when we are, we isolate ourselves.

Today, I am flexible and I am capable of adapting to all of life's situations.

July 15

What School Doesn't Teach Us

There can be no doubt that education is a precious asset that can contribute significantly to our success. But many of the lessons we learn are not taught to us in school, but in everyday life. A couple is confronted with the very real demands of life in a relationship and in a family. Both partners must learn to work as a team while also respecting each other's desires and expectations. If we want to experience true happiness, learning these lessons is crucial.

Each day brings us the opportunity of learning a new lesson. When we are open to life's lessons, we experience life optimistically and enthusiastically. A relationship teaches us new ways to act and new ways to see things. When we are open to such lessons, we fulfill our fundamental mission of living life as part of a couple.

Today, I am open and receptive to the lessons life can teach me.

Other People's Opinions

Everybody has opinions on relationships. Often, these opinions can be very interesting and they can prove to be very useful. People can tell us when we should be tender and when we should be firm, how to raise our children, how to solve relationship problems and what to serve at breakfast. But there is a significant difference between the person who is sharing an actual experience and the person who is simply formulating an opinion. Opinions can be found on every street corner, but the advice of someone who has built a successful relationship is worth much more.

We can be interested in hearing different opinions. They can be stimulating and they can help us look at things from different angles. But in the final analysis, we should never base our decisions on opinions. Rather, we should seek to deepen our knowledge by doing our own analyses and by experiencing situations directly.

Today, I know that opinions can be interesting, but I must discover my own solutions.

July 17

Love's Instruction Manual

"For a long time, I looked for a manual on how relationships worked. I wanted a guidebook to help me understand and improve my ability to create a happy and positive relationship. There are many interesting approaches to life and there are an almost infinite quantity of books on personal development. But I've discovered that the only way to find answers to our questions is by working together. We can definitely find inspiration in the theories and strategies put forward by great thinkers, but we have to find our own truths and our own way in life."

— Paul D.

Today, I know that I can rely on my own good judgement and my own intelligence to build a solid and happy relationship.

JULY 18

Walk a Mile in My Shoes

"Tolerance is the charitable expression of intelligence."

— JULES LEMAÎTRE

Tolerance is giving other people the right to be, to have their own ideas, customs and beliefs, to like whatever reflects their own tastes and to live and think differently that me.

Tolerance begins at the core of any society: the family. It begins with parents who watch their toddlers taking their very first steps, who patiently share their knowledge and their life experience, who encourage their children and teach them to be perseverant. Children need time to learn and understand; knowledge and wisdom is something acquired gradually. Children remember precisely what we say and how we say it. As proof, think of the hatred that is passed down from generation to generation in some instances.

Today, I see that I must be tolerant because I want to cooperate with others and I want to live in harmony. Team work is crucial to success; I am open to different ideas, personalities and ways of being.

July 19

The Terms and Conditions for Satisfaction

Couples should set down the terms and conditions for satisfaction. The process consists of defining what will make my partner feel happy and satisfied and what she expects from me; it means clearly defining what I expect from our relationship and how I can be happy and satisfied within our couple. Of course, we may encounter unexpected circumstances along the way and when we do, we can renegotiate. But by setting the terms for our satisfaction, we can grow together, with peace of mind, because we both know what is expected of us. This exercise also makes us aware of our shared and individual needs.

Today, along with my partner, I will define the terms and conditions for a satisfying relationship.

July 20

Going Further

"If at first you don't succeed, try, try again."
— Boileau

Persevere is a word whose stem comes from the Latin for "severe" (severus), meaning inflexible. Someone who is perseverant never quits. People who have been successful in their lives all have something in common: perseverance. Their success stories show consistent effort, persistence in difficult situations and the will to go on, even when the temptation to give in to discouragement must have been very great.

The success of our relationship depends on our perseverance. People who have spent 10, 20, 30 or 40 years together have persevered. They made the conscious decision to stay together regardless of events or circumstances. They went through hard times together. They used life's difficulties to grow closer and to strengthen their relationship. Today, we tend to believe that we'll stay together only as long as we are happy. This idea already holds the seeds of failure and breakup. To make our relationship a success, we need the determination to stay together no matter what life brings us.

Today, I understand that perseverance comes from within; I cannot find it elsewhere. Even if friends encourage me, nothing can replace my own perseverance.

JULY 21

Being Genuine

"Strength is expressed through ferocious honesty with oneself. Only when one has the courage to face things as they are, without illusion or deception, can the light of truth spring forth to guide us on the right path."

— THE I CHING

Honesty is a quality associated with individuals who refuse to rob or cheat others. However, originally the word was associated with the notion of honor. Someone honest was someone just, worthy of consideration and esteem.

Honesty is a vital quality that we must possess if we want our relationship to be successful. Firstly, we must be ferociously honest with ourselves. We must see things as they are and we must be able to rely on ourselves. We must know that we always do what has to be done and we must know that we always keep our word. We must have the ability to face difficult situations and problems with no hesitation, knowing that we can find the best possible solution. In addition, by being honest and sincere with our partner, we earn respect and trust. By being honest, we create emotional stability and security within the couple. Our partner knows who we are and how reliable we are.

Today, I know that honesty and frankness are crucial values.

Creating Harmony

"Our lives are punctuated with kind words and gracious gestures. We feed on expressions marking basic courtesy, such as: "Excuse me, please." Impoliteness (the negation of the sacrament of consideration) is yet another characteristic of our society, focused on money, deprived of spirituality, perhaps even deprived of the pleasure of living."

— ED HAYS

All individuals want to live in happiness and harmony. Sometimes we forget that courtesy begins with ourselves. We can take our partner for granted and we can believe that no matter what we say or do, he or she will always be with us. But courtesy serves to soften human relationships and to make them more pleasant. We can use courtesy to show our partner our respect and love. Courtesy contributes to a couple's enjoyment of life and it helps create emotional stability. When we neglect courtesy, communication within the couple can begin to deteriorate quickly. By being polite and courteous, I contribute to the quality of my relationship and I avoid conflicts and misunderstandings.

Today, I am courteous to my partner. By being courteous, I demonstrate my sensitivity and my respect.

What Do I Expect from My Relationship?

It can be interesting to look at what each partner expects from life in a relationship. Each person can ask themselves what they truly want in the relationship. By clearly defining our expectations, we are in an ideal position to grasp the type of experience and the type of relationship we want to build together. Starting from the principle that we can maintain precisely the kind of relationship we want, we can create and negotiate every single aspect of our life together. There is no need to base our relationship on a series of compromises or to accept the status quo.

We can define clearly what we expect from life as part of a couple. We can determine the type of couple we want and we can create the life we want together. We can set aside for good the endless compromises based on the perception that we can never have what we truly want. We can also set aside for good the notion that we must live an "acceptable" life. Together, we can pursue our dreams and we can shape our life to reflect our needs.

Today, I can communicate what I expect from our relationship. I can also be receptive to my partner's needs.

Taking Position

To make our relationship a success, we must take position. If we think that we can start something and end it along the way if we see that it isn't what we expected, we will never make a full commitment and we will never reach our objectives. Success calls for an unwavering and unconditional commitment. We must take position and say: "I am here until the end, no matter what." It's a matter of determination and more importantly, of total commitment. When I take position and decide to move forward, I send a powerful message to the universe as a whole. If I reserve the possibility of backing out or giving up, I send an equally powerful message to the entire universe.

Today, I take position by deciding to pursue my relationship.

Succeeding Step by Step

"Today, I know that before I can run, I have to learn to walk. When I want to achieve a specific objective, I know that I have to go about it one step at a time. In business, a common reason for failure is trying to do things too quickly and in the mean time, skipping important steps. Success involves gradual progress based on consolidation. I must move forward gradually, completing each step of my project before I begin the next one. Consolidation requires that the next action I take in a project rest on building blocks I have laid down during previous steps. I create stability when I complete each individual step of a project carefully and meticulously."

— Success, One Day at a Time

We entertain the false perception that once we've found our partner, our lives will magically change and we will be happy forever. The life experience of the couple teaches us otherwise. We must build our relationship step by step. The reward is knowing that we can live together and contribute to the happiness of at least one other person. Some people have more natural ability to succeed in their relationship than others but, each individual can create a happy relationship by agreeing to be present in the couple and by agreeing to grow, to learn and to adapt within it.

Today, I know that I can build a successful relationship if I learn to proceed step by step.

JULY 26

Strength and Weakness

"Through sheer luck, a man may reign over the world for a little while; but by virtue of love and goodness, he can reign over the world forever."

— LAO-TZU

Many people still don't understand that it is impossible to dominate, control or enslave people using force and aggression. Our societies are increasingly violent and we attempt to settle our differences by using intimidation and violence. Violence breeds violence. Force leads to a reaction of equal magnitude. Such is the structure of the universe. Only goodness, kindness and compassion can tear down the walls that separate us.

Today, I see that goodness is the path that leads to the highest levels of consciousness and action. I turn away from intimidation and aggression and I adopt the attitudes and behaviors based on love and compassion.

July 27

Loving, Learning and Growing

"We who have lived in concentration camps remember people who gave comfort to others, along with their last morsel of bread. Perhaps they are few in number, but they are the proof that you can rob a man of everything save one: the last of human freedoms, the freedom to choose his attitude, regardless of the circumstances, to choose his path."

— Victor Frankl

We have the choice of living a life of greatness or a life of smallness. We have all the elements at hand to make enlightened choices. We can choose to be good, honest and sincere or we can choose to be selfish, indifferent and superficial. We can choose between the superficial world of appearances or the world of truth and light. We are not here to accumulate material wealth or to honor our physical bodies. We are here to love, to learn and to grow.

We can undertake the manifestation of goodness and love within a couple because we live within it. By showing tenderness and kindness to the person who shares our intimacy, we set out a signal to the universe: I know how to love; I know how to live with compassion and affinity.

Today, I choose to live life on a higher level and I show that I am capable of loving and living with compassion.

July 28

Total Commitment

"A life united with mine, for the rest of our days... Such is the miracle of marriage!"

— Denis de Rougemont

Marriage is a total and permanent commitment. Marriage is a sacred contract between two individuals who wish to unite, because in a union, life takes on a new meaning, a broader sense. Marriage is the foundation of society. It ensures the security of individuals and allows the species to procreate in a context of equilibrium. Marriage is the nucleus of the community, the parish, the city and the nation. Without marriage, our societies progressively slip into chaos and decline.

Marriage brings several rewards: it gives us emotional stability, if offers security and peace of mind, it allows us to live and to grow within a family and thus, it offers us genuine connectedness in life, it gives us allies, it protects us against society's dangerous elements, it gives us personal discipline and family discipline, marriage offers us greater financial security. In addition to filling our basic needs for love, sexuality and security, marriage allows us to build strategic alliances and extend our sphere of influence. Those who believe that marriage is a symbol of imprisonment or a renouncement of individuality know nothing of the true nature of marriage.

Today, I choose you for the rest of my life.

Respecting the Rules

"What makes me furious is that I have to pay for my children's upkeep but I have none of the advantages of family life. My ex-wife demands monthly support payments. I have custody of the kids every two weekends. So I need an apartment that's big enough to accommodate them. Audrey has a new life now. She has a good job. She has a house and a car. I have to work like a slave to pay for the children and I live in a four and a half room apartment."

— BOBBY G.

There are certain rules governing relationships. Some people think that they should be even more strict since many people refuse to shoulder their responsibilities with regard to their couple, their children and their family. They are content to use their couple for their own personal gratification. Society has laws to protect the integrity of couples and the family because too many individuals refuse to honor their commitments. Relationships involve long-term responsibilities, particularly when there are children in the picture. Investing in a lasting relationship is preferable by far to crying over spilled milk. But when a relationship must come to an end, each partner must bear a fair share of the resultant responsibilities.

Today, I agree to take responsibility for my relationship and for my family, on this day and forever.

July 30

The Ideal Scenario

"You have to accept life as it comes to you, but you should try to make sure that it comes to you in just the way you'd like it."

— German saying

The couple is a context shaped by two people. The ideal scenario is the ideal context we set out to create. We can move closer or further from the ideal scenario. When we move closer to it, we recognize it because we've already imagined it. When we move away from it, we must take immediate action to rectify the situation. Today, we can use our resources, our talents and our imagination to create the ideal scenario.

We can passively accept what life brings us, or in light of the prevailing reality, we can work to create a context that reflects our expectations and our desires. The context of my relationship is not predetermined, it is malleable.

Today, I move closer to the ideal scenario for our relationship.

July 31

Love as a Duty

"Love does not always consist of doing what we 'feel' like doing. Love is also a duty, it is what we have chosen to do because we have made a commitment to love. The duties of love lead us to go beyond the impulse of momentary feelings and to do what love commands us to do rather than what it makes us feel like doing."

— Daphne Rose Kingma

Each individual in society has a code of moral conduct. The couple gives us an opportunity to develop a personal code of ethics that will prevail permanently, to the benefit of our survival and our well-being. Fundamentally, the duties of the couple are the moral responsibilities that we have toward our partner to ensure that the relationship survives. The couple requires a physical, emotional and moral presence on the part of both partners. Each gesture we make that contributes to the harmony, growth and prosperity of the couple brings the reward of personal satisfaction, pride and self-fulfillment.

Today, I welcome the moral, physical and emotional duties of our relationship.

August 1

Being a Source of Inspiration

"When I met Tommy, he was very active, he was a champion tennis player and a very good hockey player. Besides his work and a very active social life, he followed the Stock Market and was interested in politics. After our marriage, and especially after the birth of our first child, Tommy sank into a very routine existence. He stopped playing sports and he dropped his other interests and structured his whole life around his job and the family. I never understood why he gave up the activities that made his life so full."

— Nancy G.

When some people start a relationship, they think: "That's it! Now that I have emotional security I can rest." The relationship becomes a hiding place and a refuge from life. It becomes enough to take care of the basics, and nothing more. But the basics aren't enough; we should reach beyond minimal expectations and we should always continue to move forward. Anything that stands still eventually begins to decay and disappear. By being a source of inspiration for my partner, by being dynamic and interested in life, I can ensure the survival and growth of our relationship.

Today, I will not fall into the trap of a routine life. I know that growth is vital. By being active and by taking on new projects, I can be a source of inspiration for my partner.

AUGUST 2

The Principle of Non-Action

In his book, the Tao-ti-Chin, Lao-Tzu outlines the virtues of non-action. Non-action is the ability to wait, to observe, to listen and to explore before acting. Each event is driven by its own dynamics in relation to the laws of the universe. At times, the biggest mistake we can make is to take action instead of letting things take their course. The impatient individual is unable to take the time to explore; he rushes headlong into action and as a result, upsets the natural order of things. There is an important message here. Action must be in harmony with the situation and at times, not taking action and letting events take their course is the best decision.

There is a special type of dynamics within a relationship and it results from the concerted effort of two spiritual beings seeking to survive and to express themselves. The dynamics of a relationship can take the form of a graceful dance or an endless scramble. By being receptive to the dynamics inherent in my relationship, I can adjust accordingly. When I attempt to impose my own personal dynamics, I can only upset the equilibrium within my relationship. I must learn to look and to listen before I act.

Today, I no longer seek to rush things, instead, I am in harmony with the natural laws that govern the relationships between human beings.

AUGUST 3

Major Victories

The road to love and genuine commitment is filled with minor and major victories. Each day brings us minor victories: shared activities, loving words and gestures that warm the heart and small favors that please. We must also celebrate major victories: being together and communicating despite stress and conflict within the relationship, the birth of a healthy child, a quality of life improved as a result of a special effort, success in a career, another wedding anniversary celebrated together. By focusing our attention on victories instead of defeats, we have a better chance of making our relationship successful. Life is punctuated with events, some are positive, others are negative. But if we look for victories, we see that over time, a relationship becomes more dynamic and less demanding. Together, we succeed each and every day. Together, we can celebrate minor and major victories.

Today, I enjoy our small victories and I look forward to our major victories.

August 4

Between Dreams and Reality

"To get the promised land, each of us must negotiate a road through the jungle."

— Herb Cohen

Between our dreams and their achievement lies a whole world. A world filled with solutions, stumbling blocks, resources, barriers and many other factors that will come into play in the material achievement of our dreams. We live in a world of constant change and each day, we should look for the advantages it brings us. We are two spiritual beings living in a material world. To maintain our love, we must deal with the prevailing reality. Today, we can make our dreams come true. Our shared will to make them come true is stronger than the reality we live in. Together, we can impose our view of the world and we can experience anything we choose. We set out with the idea that we can make all of our projects successful and we can find solutions to all of our problems.

Today, I feel that I can overcome any obstacles on my path. Together, we can live a happy and fulfilling life.

One Man Among Many

"When I stayed briefly with the Wayanas, a primitive South American tribe, I was surprised to see the type of relationships there were between men and women. For the men of the tribe, all women were the same. And for the women in the tribe, all men were the same. They saw no difference between individuals and they show no preference for any one individual. As far as relationships go, one man is as good as any other and as attractive as any other. I realized that our concepts of romantic love — based mainly on finding the one person who is for us — are entirely fabricated."

— GENE F.

Our culture emphasizes the need to select an ideal partner. If we think we've made the wrong choice, we begin to look for the right person all over again. We attach a great deal of importance to the cult of individuality and difference. Obviously, we do not live in the context of a primitive tribe. But our obsession with the person who is perfectly and absolutely suited for us blinds us to real situations. When I live in the hope of meeting that one person on earth who is for me and me alone, I am not present for those who do love me and for the person who could, over time, become the person for me.

Today, I know that the person I am looking for is already in my environment.

Criticism

"Instead of condemning people, we should try to understand them. We should try to understand why they do the things they do. Understanding is much more positive and profitable than criticism and it generates much more sympathy, tolerance and benevolence."

— DALE CARNEGIE

In everyday life, we encounter many unexpected situations. We often wonder about people's motivations and behaviors. Sometimes, someone around us does something that truly upsets us, that seems to stop us from being able to reach our objectives, or that makes it hard to be happy. Although we may want to reach angrily or impatiently, the best approach is take time out to calm down. Harsh criticism is never constructive and is never an acceptable solution.

Most of the time, the person who has hurt us, thought that he or she was doing nothing wrong. Through dialogue and exchange, we can build lasting ties of mutual help. Criticism generates only misunderstanding and it is always less effective than constructive dialogue.

Today, I believe in constructive dialogue and I realize that harsh criticism can only have a harmful and very negative effect.

AUGUST 7

Knowing Ourselves

"Harvey and I got married when we were 19. Our families and friends pressured us into getting married. I think we would have been happy to continue dating for a while longer and then we could have lived together before taking the big step. Our marriage didn't last very long. I think it destroyed what had been a beautiful relationship. We woke up one day and realized that we had more responsibilities than either of us wanted and we were overwhelmed with the problems we encountered in our new life together."

— SOPHIE L.

Before making a commitment, we must get to know the other person, but more importantly we must get to know ourselves. Most of the time, deciding to share a lifetime with another person calls for mental and emotional preparations that take several months, even years. Some people need a series of experiences before they feel ready to make a definite commitment to a relationship. Throughout our lives, we learn more and more about ourselves; we come to know our expectations, our desires, our strengths and our weaknesses. At some point in time, we know ourselves sufficiently well to trust our own choices. Some individuals reach this level of maturity before others.

Today, I understand the importance of preparing carefully for any long-term undertaking.

Looking for Love in All the Wrong Places

"I spent most of my adult life looking for love instead of creating love. I mistakenly though that if I looked actively for a partner, I would end up finding one. I used to go to bars. I used to go to singles' meetings. I used to look for group activities to meet as many people as I could. My active approach certainly led to a number of encounters and to several liaisons as well. But the women I met weren't really the type of women I was looking for. And when I least expected it, when I'd stopped looking, I did meet someone special. I was sitting quietly in my own living room when she rang the doorbell. Madeleine was conducting a poll. I fell in love at first sight."

— CHARLES L.

Our intentions do more to determine our future than our gestures do. When I intend to meet my partner and when I prepare my heart to welcome that person into my life, I send a powerful signal to the universe. An intention is not a desire or a hope, it is the certitude that sooner or later, I will reach my objective. When I intend to reach a goal and when my intention is unshakable, nothing can keep me from it.

Today, I intend to experience a wonderful relationship.

Loving Unreservedly and Unconditionally

In each one of us lays the profound desire to love and to be loved. Perhaps we are but pure love seeking a way to manifest itself: perhaps social conventions, the dangers of society and the corruption of love through suppression, all lead us to hide our true nature. We see this true nature in children, who love spontaneously, who never hold back their love. Their affection and their desire to communicate is so pure and so constant that it can be disarming. We remember being like them not so long ago, when we were able to give our love unreservedly and unconditionally.

Today, I am in contact with my true nature. I love unreservedly and unconditionally because I myself am love.

August 10

Seeing Through Other People's Eyes

"The biggest secret to success is the ability to see things through the other person's eyes and to look at things from a different angle than your own point of view."

— Henry Ford

Each person has their own preoccupations and their own desires. If, to serve my own purposes, I insist on trying to persuade other people that they should see things my way, I will be bitterly disappointed. I must develop the ability to see what other people want and to look at things as they see them. I will win their support if I can help them reach their own objectives.

Today, I know that if I want to sell a product or a service to someone, I must have the ability to fill their needs and to meet their expectations. I must listen carefully to their objections and their concerns if I want to be persuasive. The same holds true in my interaction with my partner.

August 11

The Greatest Reward

"Tell people how good you feel when they do something well and how much it means to the organization and to their colleagues."

— K. Blanchard and S. Johnson

When things are going well, they're easy to take for granted. We are happy living together and we are convinced that the other person knows how much we love and value them. We exchange gifts on birthdays and anniversaries. We go out and we call each other during the day, but we forget the most important thing: the greatest reward is being appreciated and receiving verbal recognition for our qualities. We forget the essential: recognizing aloud and sincerely how much we appreciate our partner.

Today, I take the time to give compliments, to express my appreciation and to encourage my partner.

August 12

Ending a Negative Relationship

A love relationship, like a professional relationship, should be founded on integrity, communication and reciprocal interest. Before becoming involved in a relationship, we must be able to trust the other person and we ourselves must be worthy of trust. When we feel let down, we should determine the reason. Most situations and most problems can be resolved with frank and open dialogue. However, if the situation that is worrying me persists despite reassuring words, I must react.

We may believe ending a relationship will leave us alone and depressed. In the short term, this may be true. But in the long run, we will feel happier for having eliminated a source of unhappiness and betrayal.

Today, I know that I must end relationships that are negative. My mental and emotional well-being and equilibrium are my priorities.

August 13

Wiping the Slate Clean

Day-to-day life brings us into contact with many people who harbor resentment toward a colleague, an acquaintance or a family member. The feeling can last for days, months and even years. We all know someone who cannot or will not forgive and who poison their lives with bitterness and resentment.

A love relationship requires that we be willing to wipe the slate clean in certain instances. We must accept and forgive transgressions, big and small alike. Without the ability to forgive, a relationship becomes a living hell.

Today, I forgive.

August 14

Taking Courses Together

Why not take a course together? You can register for swimming, dancing, pottery, computer software, motivational or language courses, the list is virtually unlimited. When a couple follows a course together, they learn, they meet new people, they get away from their ordinary routines and they share a specific objective and activity. Each partner in a couple needs outside stimulation. By taking a course together, you increase your knowledge in a field of interest to both of you and you have the satisfaction of accomplishing something together.

Today, I see that life is a learning process. Why not do something practical and enjoyable by taking a course together?

AUGUST 15

What Can I Do for You

"Ask not what your country can do for you. Ask what you can do for your country."

— JOHN F. KENNEDY

To make a relationship successful, I should ask not what it can do for me, but what I can do for it. A relationship is a cooperative effort. Instead of focusing on my own needs, I focus my attention on my partner's needs and our needs as a couple. By doing so, I find new solutions to the problems involved in most relationships.

Generally, people are preoccupied mainly by their own needs; the needs of others are of relatively little interest. Being in a relationship calls for a 180-degree change in this perception. The couple's needs and the other person's needs should be more important to me than my individual needs. The couple's needs and the other person's needs should become my own needs. Together, we look at life as a couple.

Today, my priorities are my partner's needs and our needs as a couple.

Each Person is Important

School doesn't necessarily teach us that we should be interested in others. But our sincere interest in other people is often a determinant factor in our lives. Everyone is preoccupied by their own fate and is familiar mainly with their own desires and their own needs. However, to make a relationship successful, I must be interested in my partner. I must have the ability of seeing things from my partner's point of view as well as my own. I must show my sincere interest in my partner, my partner's needs and my partner's expectations.

Today, I am sincerely interested in my partner and I show my interest.

AUGUST 17

Feelings are Like a Tide

Like waves on a beach, feelings come, and then they go. We can cling to one feeling in particular, or we can let it come and go. We can feel sad, melancholic or angry. Feelings come over us suddenly. We can act according to our feelings. We can also let them come and go without focusing on them. And when they go, calmness returns. Instead of resisting feelings, we should welcome and embrace them.

Today, I embrace all of my feelings and I welcome them.

August 18

When Love Fades

"I was in love when I got married 20 years ago. But now, there's no more love in our couple. We still live together, but by necessity and force of habit. We have sex now and then, but by duty, not by inclination. When we do, I think of someone else and I know he does too. Our relationship is a financial arrangement that we tolerate; it's far from a union based on love and intimacy."

— Irene T.

Life in a couple can be a prison. Two individuals who hurt each other and who are suffering can choose to abandon the relationship and withdraw into their own space. The conditions that prevail in society in general don't always make it easy for a couple to separate. And so we agree to live under difficult circumstances rather than end up alone and helpless. But as long as there is life, there is hope. It is possible to revitalize a dead relationship. Of course, the task is enormous. But the power of love and communication can break down walls of steel. By opening our hearts, in spite of the pain of the past, we may find deep inside ourselves the vestiges of love. By making the effort of facing the situation as it is, we can find the energy to start all over again or to end the relationship once and for all. Love is precious. No one should accept a relationship where love and passion are absent.

Today, I refuse to live in a relationship without love and passion.

August 19

Small Gestures

"Thoughtfulness, that most wonderful of products of the human heart, expresses itself most effectively in small gestures."

— Mary Botham Howitt

The word "courteous" is the oldest adjective connected to the notion of politeness. It comes to us from the Middle Ages, which marked a new lifestyle different from the lifestyle typical of the warriors of the time. Courteous was used to describe a refinement in behavior and sensibility. So it could be said that politeness and courtesy were invented to make the world a gentler, more beautiful place.

Courtesy involves very simple gestures: taking time to say hello to someone; letting someone go ahead of you when you're waiting in line. You don't have to be rich to be courteous. Polite behavior knows no boundaries related to age or money.

Today, I see that courtesy between partners in a relationship creates an atmosphere of harmony and respect.

AUGUST 20

Gentleness

"I believe that humanity will not only last, it will prevail. Man is immortal, not because of all creatures he is the only one with an indefatigable voice, but because he has a soul, a spirit capable of goodness and compassion."

— WILLIAM FAULKNER

Gentleness will always be more piercing, more penetrating than brute force. Just as water shows its force in the fact that it has no resistance but can still grind stone into sand, the greatest victories are won with gentleness. Gentleness lets me overcome and eliminate all resistance.

The smile of a small child, the silky coat of a purring cat, the light springtime breeze, the caress of a loved one — all are images that evoke gentleness. Gentleness is to the soul what grace is to gesture. Harshness and vulgarity should have no place in a life built on harmony.

Today, I use gentleness to break down the walls that keep us apart.

August 21

Stress

As we try to find our way on the road to success, we may experience times of particularly acute stress. Financial problems, deadlines, production or management errors, personal conflicts or conflicts with colleagues, economic cycles that threaten the very survival of our companies or tax audits that can cause upheaval in our business operations are only a few examples of the stressful situations that can affect an individual. It is very hard to feel good when we are preoccupied or stressed.

There is no miracle solution to stress. On the other hand, the worst response to stress is the use of alcohol and drugs to try to lessen the anxiety that can come with stressful situations. It is always preferable to solve problems that cause anxiety and stress by keeping a clear mind and by taking good care of myself. Life is filled with different situations, some more stressful than others. We must learn to manage stress and to use it to our advantage.

Today, I know that I must face life's stressful situations without transferring my anxiety and my frustration to my partner. By learning to solve problems and by managing my stress effectively, I can protect our relationship.

Emotional Support

"No one can live his life solely for himself. Thousands of strings tie us to our brothers; intertwined in these strings, such as feelings of compassion, our actions are transmuted into causes and return to us as effects."

— HERMAN MELVILLE

Today, I can accept my partner's help and emotional support. By allowing my partner to give me emotional support, I am open to the special sharing in our relationship.

AUGUST 23

The Power of Reconciliation

"I think that our relationship has lasted this long because we know how to reconcile. We have undergone major difficulties: unfaithfulness, financial problems, job losses, etc. But we have always been able to forgive each other and ourselves for past mistakes. We consider our relationship as much more important than the events in our lives. We are prepared to take on life's tests together. Sometimes I'm the one who needs to be forgiven or to fix a mistake. Sometimes Ann-Marie does or says something that I think is unacceptable. I've learned to wipe the slate clean. In my heart of hearts, I know that she is the woman I want to grow old with. Our problems have made us stronger. We have learned how powerful reconciliation can be in a relationship."

— IVAN M.

Reconciliation is the power to forgive, even when forgiving is painful. Reconciliation is knowing that a relationship is worth saving despite the hurt or the pain that we may have suffered. Reconciliation is making peace in the truest sense of the term, with no lingering feelings of resentment or bitterness. A couple cannot survive without reconciliation.

Today, I see that reconciliation is vital. When I am hurt, I agree to share my feelings with my partner.

AUGUST 24

Respecting Differences

"The person you love will not see your love or your relationship in exactly the same way as you. He or she may have very different feelings on which direction the relationship should go in, on how to discuss things, on how and when to make love, and even on the meaning of the word relationship."

— DAPHNE ROSE KINGMA

Today, I recognize and respect the differences between my partner and me.

AUGUST 25

Simplicity

"All we need to feel happy can be found here and now — all we need is a simple heart."

— NIKOS KAZANTZAKIS

Without denying the importance of past events that may have been painful and traumatic, I do not think that we are inevitably chained to the demons of our past. Believing that we are would amount to saying that we are puppets, incapable of controlling our own destiny. When we lead positive and healthy lives and when we apply authentic values such as honesty, respect and loyalty in our day-to-day dealings, life is much simpler. It is true that life is filled with obstacles and at times we feel the burden of past failures. But if we show determination and if we remain faithful to our principles, we run much less risk of falling into depression and anxiety. In a relationship, it is important to remain open to reconciliation and to rid our lives of annoyances. By refusing all forms of bitterness and animosity, we can experience the joy of a light heart and a mind open to all things positive.

Today, I renounce bitterness and past grudges and I open my heart to my partner.

August 26

Difficult Days

Anyone who is a partner in a relationship knows that there are days when things go wrong. We find it hard to stand the other person's presence and we would prefer to be alone. When this type of day comes along, we tend to argue for no apparent reason, we refuse to cooperate in even the smallest ways and we practise passive resistance. We sometimes even feel that the other person wants us to be unhappy.

When such situations occur, we should try to step back and avoid letting our stormy feelings overwhelm us. We should ask for our partner's help to weather the turbulence and we should attempt to behave in a gentler and more understanding way. This is a time to take good care of ourselves, to pamper ourselves until we feel better. A stroll in the park, a bubble bath, a nap — three small tactics that can go a long way. We should be aware that conflicts and arguments usually occur when we don't feel quite right. Such times are perfect times to spoil ourselves a little and to make a point of avoiding tricky situations.

Today, I can weather stormy days with hope and courage.

AUGUST 27

Finding Love

"Too many people imagine that to find love, they have to advertise in singles' columns, cruise in bars or consult dating agencies. These activities may have their raison d'être, but it is important not to neglect the interior aspects of our preparation — by far the most important and precisely those which we neglect most often. Love that is true and deep, love that lasts a lifetime will not manifest itself because of exterior activities, but because you have unlocked the emotional and spiritual doors that prevent love from entering your life."

— DAPHNE ROSE KINGMA

Today, I unlock the doors to my heart and I welcome true love into my life.

Encouraging

The effect of criticism is easy to see on someone's face. When we criticize or argue with our partner, he or she withdraws and closes off. Another reaction may be aggressive behavior or criticism directed back at us as a means of protection and defense. Criticism inevitably leads to detachment and conflict. It is easy to see that criticism does very little to motivate people to improve in any way. Criticism is often the first reaction we have when faced with something that displeases us. This first reaction is rarely the right reaction because it is neither constructive nor well thought out.

Today, I prefer to encourage rather than criticize. Instead of reacting spontaneously and criticizing, I take a few minutes to reflect on the situation. I try to understand it as best I can and I use words of encouragement to motivate my partner.

AUGUST 29

Two Lives

"When we began to going out together, I made the mistake of accepting a principle I disagreed with. Jake wanted to keep social contacts and do activities outside of the relationship and he encouraged me to do likewise. According to him, the relationship could last if each of us had a rich and active life outside the couple. This way, we'd never feel imprisoned in the relationship and we'd never feel that our space was being invaded. I wanted to be with him so much that I agreed to these terms although they seemed to be the complete opposite of my idea of life as a happy couple. I told myself that with time, he'd adopt a more sedentary lifestyle and he'd want to spend his free time with me. After a few years, I realized that we had two separate lives. I spent evenings alone, worrying and wondering if he was really interested in me."

— CHRISTINE S.

We cannot betray one of our basic principles without being aware of the betrayal. However, we may think that such a compromise is the only way to save a relationship. But compromising on something so fundamental rarely leads to happiness. The best path by far is to remain loyal to our principles and to listen to our inner selves.

Today, I know the difference between cooperation and compromise. I refuse to betray my basic principles in an attempt to save a relationship.

Letting Others Love You

Vulnerability hasn't always been viewed as a desirable quality. We know that when we are vulnerable, we may be hurt. When we expose our limitations and our weaknesses, we can easily fall victim to someone else. And so, many of us have learned not to be vulnerable. But there is another side to vulnerability: the ability to ask for help and love and the potential to receive both. In this sense, vulnerability is an openness and a receptiveness.

Today, I prepare my heart to give and to receive love. I have always found it easier to love than to be loved. I thought that this way, I could stay in control of the situation. But now, I see that this approach cannot work.

August 31

Giving the Best of Yourself

Sincerity and the will to contribute to the well-being of our relationship are visible things. Sincerity is vital to a relationship. We need to know that the other person is interested in us and in the couple. We must also show our sincere interest in our partner's well-being through our attentiveness and the gestures we make. With good will and frank exchange, we can travel on life's road together.

Today, I give the best of myself to my partner.

September 1

The Rhythm of Love

Each relationship nurtures its needs and its expectations. Like a flower garden, a relationship requires the attention and care of a gardener. Modern life often takes us away from our families to take care of professional or business imperatives. We work extremely hard, sparing no effort and not counting the hours we put in, to ensure our families subsistence and as a result, we relegate those we love to a secondary place in our lives. We run the risk of drifting further and further apart from those we love, eventually losing sight of the needs felt within our relationship. Yet financial success is worthless unless we can share it with loved ones. To build a balanced and lasting relationship requires time, energy and passion. We must also respect our partner and be willing to adapt to his or her needs and rhythm.

Today, I know that by being present I can experience and enjoy our relationship to the fullest.

Being Right or being Wrong

Most conflicts in a relationship result from the fact that we think we are right and the other person is wrong. We dig our heels in and refuse to yield. A relationship calls for much more flexibility and awareness than that. No one likes to admit they're wrong or to be told repeatedly that they're wrong. This reaction stems from personal pride. No one appreciates being subjected to domination or criticism. When we are faced with this type of situation, we should try to understand the other person's opinion, instead of automatically making a point of voicing ours. It is equally important to maintain a cordial approach at all times. With a bit of objectivity, most conflicts can be resolved.

Today, I know that I can be right and I can be wrong. I can see things from my partner's standpoint and I can adapt to the reality of our relationship.

SEPTEMBER 3

Love is Everywhere

"Some poeple say that the best way to attract love is to develop our ability to love. Love is all around us, as each person has the ability and the desire to love and to be loved. Love is incarnated in each human being we encounter.

Although we may be having some difficulty in finding the love of our life, we may console ourselves in the fact that love is like honey and, ultimately, will attrack love."

— ANONYMOUS

Today, I see that love is everywhere. By developing my ability to love and to be loved, I find strength in the source of universal love and I am transformed.

SEPTEMBER 4

The Religious Foundation of the Couple

"I had lost all religious faith until I go married. Our parents insisted on a traditional church wedding and we agreed for the sake of keeping the peace. The preparations and the religious ceremony revived my faith. I felt that God would be with us throughout our marriage; I felt that the marriage was a spiritual union before God. Marriage is more than a simple relationship between two people. I see marriage as a moral and spiritual contract entered into with God's consent and support."

— SARAH G.

Many people turn away from religion on the pretext that is is a form of exploitation based on mystery and blind faith. But we've also turned away from its positive aspects: a moral code founded on goodness, a relationship with God, religious rites that remind us that we are spiritual beings, not just physical bodies. The couple is a union that is spiritual in nature. We can do without the help of God, Jesus, Buddha or Allah throughout a lifetime, but life is richer when we provide ourselves with a framework from within which we can express our spiritual drives and needs.

Today, I feel that my relationship is the result of the spiritual nature of the ties that bind us. I can celebrate these spiritual ties today and every day.

SEPTEMBER 5

Putting an End to Suffering!

"I fell in love with suffering. My relationship was hell and suffering confirmed my beliefs. I was born to suffer, and by suffering, I was earning salvation. My husband did some terrible things. He tried to hurt me and I think that I encouraged him because I felt that I deserved to be punished. From the outset, I knew that he would make my life a living hell and I was strongly attracted by the promise of suffering and hardship. I cried an ocean of tears before realizing that I was entertaining purely false notions. Suffering has no therapeutic value. Suffering doesn't make me better, more spiritual or bring closer to God. Suffering is nothing but a sign of my unhappiness."

— SONIA B.

When we are hurt or suffering, we don't always know how to find happiness again. The road to happiness begins when I knowingly decide not to live with an individual who intentionally wants to hurt or humiliate me. Even if we have no clear idea on what can make us happy, we can remove from our lives all sources of suffering and sadness. There should be no room for suffering in a relationship. A relationship should be a place where we feel secure and happy.

Today, I realize that love and suffering can never go together. I can build a relationship that brings me peace of mind and security and I can do so without suffering.

The Gift is Me!

We can live through a variety of experiences and we can take years before realizing that we deserve a happy relationship. Mistakenly, we may feel that conflict and confusion are a part of sharing our lives with someone else. When we do, arguing and going to bed angry may seem normal.

Today, I know that I deserve better. I know that I can build a happy and positive relationship. I know that I am a unique human being with qualities and intelligence, and I deserve a wonderful relationship.

Thinking "Win-Win"

A relationship calls for a "win-win" approach. Within a couple, each partner must find what he or she is looking for. If the situation is founded on giving one person the advantage over the other, the result will be dissatisfaction and bitterness. I seek to structure our relationship on the "win-win" principle.

Today, I know that by acting according to the "win-win" principle, I can build a lasting relationship. To practise this concept, I must be both firm and flexible. I must find the right balance between what is vital for me and what is vital for my partner.

September 8

Virtuous Action

In virtuous attitudes and behaviors there is a superior logic, a road that leads directly to serenity, freedom and success. But along the way, we have forgotten or lost from sight the value inherent in virtues. We have seen in goodness, kindness, compassion or gallantry something old-fashioned or outdated, no longer suited to modern life. But virtues can never be outdated because they indicate the path to salvation, divinity and success. Virtuous attitudes and behaviors are as many tangible manifestations of the true self, around which they seem to create an aura of dazzling light.

Today, I know that virtuous action holds within it the promise of success, because it opens a path from the heart to the material world of concrete achievements.

September 9

Your Loved One is Not You

We sometimes forget that our loved ones are human beings in their own right and that they exist outside of us. They have their opinions, their expectations and their needs. A love relationship can create a feeling of symbiosis. I may feel that my partner and I are one and the same person. This feeling of symbiosis may lead me to make choices without consulting my partner, thinking that in any event I am acting in our best interests. The couple is the union of two distinct individuals who each have their respective qualities. Both partners must be in constant communication and must consult each other on all matters. We must tell our partner what we like and what we dislike. Human beings change and their needs evolve with time. What was true for a long time may no longer be true at a given point. For these reasons, we must maintain active dialogue and we must enquire about our partner's wishes.

Today, I accept the fact that my partner has perceptions, wishes and expectations that are specific to him or her and they are different from my own. I see that the success of our relationship depends on my ability to respect these differences.

A Dangerous Hypothesis

"When I got married, I was convinced I would stay married for the rest of my life. Divorce and separation were both unthinkable. If we encountered difficulties or conflicts, we would find a way to overcome them. My initial hypothesis turned out to be false and I did go through a separation and a divorce. My marriage didn't last and I spent years of turmoil trying to figure out why. Today, I realize that love can last, but only if we want it to last. I am involved in a new relationship now and I think that it will withstand the test of time, but I'm careful not to take it for granted."

— RICK N.

The reality of the couple puts our initial hypothesis to the test. We may have a romantic view of the couple, but with time we come to understand that life in a relationship calls for effort and sacrifice. Day-to-day life requires constant adjustment and the ability to understand the needs of the moment. It is always dangerous to let things go and hope that they work out for the better as time goes by. We must put body and soul into a relationship with the full knowledge that there are no guarantees that it will last a lifetime. By giving the best we have, we enjoy the satisfaction of experiencing and enjoying our relationship to the fullest each day.

Today, I can question my initial hypotheses on the couple. I can adjust to the prevailing reality in my relationship.

SEPTEMBER 11

Accepting Myself Unconditionally

"Gradually, I must accept myself as I am — with no secrets, no disguises, no falseness and no rejection of any facet of myself — and with no judgement, no condemnation or denigration of any facet of myself."

— ANONYMOUS

The key to success is accepting myself unreservedly and unconditionally. Most of us have had to face our limitations, our weaknesses and our profound aloneness. When I am confronted with the person I am, I see the true degree of my frailty and my vulnerability. From this stems the need to love myself and to accept myself. We all make mistakes. We can do things with the intention of harming our own well-being. At times we are trapped in a vicious circle of habits that contribute nothing to our welfare. By being aware that we are not infallible, we can take a more human and more generous look at others.

When we are aware of our own humanity and our partner's humanity, we can open our hearts and begin to live. By accepting ourselves and by helping our partner to accept himself or herself, we can find the harmony inherent in a good relationship.

Today, I see that if I want to experience a positive relationship, I must accept myself and I must help my partner accept himself or herself.

September 12

Ruminating

"When I think of all the things I've done, I feel angry and sad. For years, I took care of that man and his children and he always laughed at me. I can't manage to escape from my memories of life with him, the betrayals I suffered and the lies he told me. We separated eight years ago, but the emotions I feel are every bit as intense and every bit as painful as they ever were."

— Bridget H.

Many people believe that divorce or separation is the solution to relationship problems. But few people are emotionally prepared for a divorce or separation. They leave the relationship with the heavy burden of unshared communication, unexpressed feelings and bitterness. A relationship can be a dynamic place for growth and sharing when we are open, receptive and welcoming toward our partner. We can always find reasons for ending a relationship. We can also choose to stay together and weather hard times. Each partner sets out with the intention to do what is best. Each partner wants to make a contribution and wants to make life together as happy as it can be. Some people find this easier to do than others. The important thing is staying in the relationship long enough to enjoy the benefits of our efforts.

Today, I know that by staying together, we can reach our objectives.

September 13

Share Your Ideal Scenario!

Each person has a specific ideal scenario for love, a specific vision of the ideal couple and how the ideal couple is formed and grows. When two people have a similar scenario, there is no problem. But when their scenarios differ, several problems can occur. At the outset of the relationship, we should share our expectations and objectives to determine if we have the same vision of things and if our ideal scenarios for love are compatible.

Today, I share my ideal scenario for love with my partner and I ask about his or hers. The exchange will bring us closer and we can begin writing a scenario for two.

SEPTEMBER 14

Life Without Love

"I wonder what my life would have been like without love. I wonder what my life would have been like if I had lived alone, if I wasn't part of a couple. I wouldn't want to live without my wife. Despite its ups and downs, I know that nothing exists outside love, outside life as part of a couple and a family. Men and women come together in the love of a couple because deep down they know that there is nothing worthwhile outside the love relationship. What can we gain from living alone?"

— STEPHEN L.

Our entire being yearns to know love and life as part of a couple. Without a love relationship, existence is superficial and mechanical. The person who is alone seeks recognition and self-knowledge in sporadic relationships. But without the dynamics of the couple, the individual has difficulty seeing the fundamental reason for life on earth. Each day, the couple reminds us that we are here to live and to work with others. The couple is the most basic form of cooperation and spiritual creation. An individual may choose to climb a mountain and meditate there to achieve the state of buddha, and this life has its merit. However, most mortals can achieve a higher level of peace and a higher level of responsibility, control and awareness by being involved in a love relationship.

Today, I know that I do not want to live without the love of a partner.

September 15

Behave Properly in Public!

"I never could stand the way she behaved in public. When she was sober, she was rather shy and reserved; but when she drank, her personality changed completely. After a few drinks, she could say the worst things and could do the unimaginable. And she felt that she had to drink to overcome her natural shyness. Our relationship didn't last because I couldn't stand being with someone who didn't know how to behave in public."

— Matthew M.

A couple must maintain a good public image. When we go out together, we must know that our partner knows how to behave in all social situations. Politeness, cordiality and affability are crucial values. What I do and what I say have an effect on the perception people have of me, of my partner and of our relationship. Good public relations lead to good social relations.

Today, I see that my behavior in public has an impact on my relationship and the perception people have of me, of my partner and of our relationship. I make a point of always being polite and likeable with the people we frequent as a couple.

Decoding Love

"After a certain number of years, I finally understood Annie better. It's not that she talked any more about her feelings or that she became more like me. When you spend a lot of time with another person and when you share their intimacy, you begin to see what makes them tick. Often before they even say a word, you know what's going on. Feelings and thoughts float through the air around us and form a kind of microclimate. The couple is a special zone. In that zone, sound waves travel freely because the barriers to true communication have been broken down. I don't always know exactly what Annie may be thinking, but I can interpret her emotional tone and I can adjust to the climate of the moment."

— SERGIO N.

Communication between two partners can be subtle. Messages are transmitted and received at a dizzying speed. A couple shares their feelings, their expectations and their aspirations. This form of authentic communication creates a climate that is specific to each couple. We have the choice to be open or closed to the communication specific to our couple. By listening to the subtle messages that travel within the context of our couple, we can learn to dance together and to live side by side.

Today, I listen to my partner's subtle messages and I maintain direct communication with him or her.

SEPTEMBER 17

Blessed by Love

"Love can lead us to a spiritual awakening. When we are in love, we can see live in a new an vibrant light. When true love touches our lives, this luminous and vibrant force fills us and give us vitality and clarity. Love is the sanctuary of our spirit, the repository of our emotions, the flowery field where we cultivate our hopes and dreams."

— ANONYMOUS

Today, I feel touched to the depths of my soul by the love and admiration I have for my partner.

SEPTEMBER 18

Much-Needed Rest

We sometimes forget that rest is crucial to happiness and well-being. We commonly ask too much of ourselves, abuse our strength and let fatigue affect our mood and our personality. The family and professional responsibilities shouldered by the partners in a relationship require a great deal of energy and when there isn't enough time for any number of duties, there isn't enough time for rest either. Fatigue leads to irritability, which in turn leads to conflict. We all know that anger is a very poor advisor and of little help in our quest for solutions to everyday problems. When we feel well rested, we are more likely to stay calm and cool under sometimes difficult circumstances. And that can only be in everyone's best interests.

Today, I am aware that rest is crucial if I want to live in happiness and harmony with my partner.

Going Through Hard Times

Every couple goes through hard times. When they last a relatively long time, we may begin to wonder if continuing in the relationship is worthwhile. At such times, life outside the couple seems to be easier and more interesting. We can easily believe that a breakup could be the solution to all our problems. But when we go through hard times together, our relationship is stronger. Perhaps human beings are particularly prone to believing that the source of their problems can be found outside themselves. We can easily convince ourselves that most of our troubles can be attributed to our partner.

Today, I know that I can go through hard times with my partner. I know that together, we are stronger and bigger than any problem we may encounter.

SEPTEMBER 20

Serving Our Partner

There is a significant difference between cooperation and subservience. A relationship should never create a climate where one partner is dominant or subservient. Each partner must be free to find fulfillment with the help and support of the other. Both partners must feel that they are loved and respected for who they are and that they can give freely. Both partners must have permission to receive and to give. Serving a partner is saying: "You are a person of great worth." I can see that serving my partner also provides me with the opportunity to receive. Each day, I take part in the flow of love that takes form in gestures and words. Each day, our relationship gives me an opportunity to participate, to serve and to receive.

Today, I will be generous. I will share with my partner. I will serve my partner without losing my identity and I will not feel exploited in any way. The dynamics of the couple allow me to exchange and share freely.

Health and Well-Being

"If I hadn't met Stephanie, I'd probably be dead today. Our relationship saved my life. I'm not proud to admit that I was a drug addict. In the job I had, drugs circulated freely and I began to take them to get more energy and to boost my self-confidence. With time, I became so dependent that I couldn't function without them. They robbed me of everything: my career as a musician, my physical and mental health, my family and all of my earthly possessions. I was uncontrollable, I was drifting out to sea. Stephanie did all she could to bring me back. But when she left me, I really touched bottom. When I lost her I finally woke up and I realized that I was about to lose everything, including my life, if I didn't do something about my addiction. I've been clean for three years now. I was so lucky! Stephanie decided to come back to me and we've built a whole new life together!"

— MICHAEL S.

Today, I see that my actions have major repercussions on our relationship. So before acting, I think and I evaluate if my action will reinforce or weaken our relationship.

Celebrating Each Small Achievement

For some people, tying their shoelaces in the morning is an achievement. Others are happy only if they reach ultimate heights. For my part, I like to celebrate small, day-to-day achievements such as working out to keep fit or eating well; succeeding in reaching an agreement with someone after a telephone conversation; reaching my sales objectives for the week. All these small achievements bring me closer to larger goals and encourage me every step of the way on my road to success.

Maintaining a stable relationship is an accomplishment in and of itself. Life as part of a couple brings with it a multitude of small and larger achievements that deserve to be underlined and celebrated. We should be proud to be together and to work together on small undertakings. We should be happy that we've decided to stay together despite pain and hardships. Each day, we should congratulate ourselves on the achievement that is our relationship.

Today, I pay attention to my achievements. I see that we have progressed and that our relationship continues to grow stronger with each passing day.

SEPTEMBER 23

Taking Time for Intimacy

We let few people enter the circle of our personal intimacy. Our partner, our parents, our immediate families and a few friends can claim that they know us well and are particularly close to us. A love relationship is undoubtedly the most intimate of all relationships because it includes all the aspects of physical, mental, emotional and spiritual intimacy. The person who chooses us to share their intimacy, must love us and respect us and take pleasure in being with us. We must consent to letting another person into our intimate circle, where we are at our most vulnerable and transparent. In the circle of intimacy that we create with a partner, we find the true emotions and the true feelings of love and pleasure.

If our relationship seems to be in turmoil, we must ask ourselves if we devote enough time and space to intimacy. Obligations and the stress of everyday life sometimes lead us to forget the world of warmth, passion and tenderness around us, close to our hearts, in the company of the person we love most in the world.

Today, I devote time to intimacy. I see that there is a world of tenderness at my fingertips.

SEPTEMBER 24

Beware the Power of Words!

We sometimes forget the power of words. A word can change the tone of a social situation. A few poorly placed words can upset a person we love. Words can build and they can destroy. Anger is often the source of words we regret, words that build walls between our loved ones and us. When we are angry, we often say hurtful words. We are convinced of being right and we are equally convinced that the other person should understand us. But when we see the effect of anger on a love relationship or any other kind of relationship, we know that it cannot lead us to harmony and happiness. In any event, words spoken in anger are generally untrue and if they contain an element of truth, the method chosen to speak them does nothing to foster understanding.

Today, I am aware of the power of words. I use words to soothe, to compliment and to strengthen the links that bind me to my loved one. And if, for whatever reason, I become angry, I am careful of the words I use because I do not want to offend.

Emphasizing the Positive

Looking at a glass that is half full, some people may describe it as half empty. They focus their attention on the emptiness and they forget the content. Other people see the same glass and describe it as half full. They see the content and forget the emptiness. Which of the two types is the happiest?

The quality of our relationship depends in large part on our perceptions. If we consider the relationship as satisfying, if we think it brings us good things and that it has the potential to make us happy until the end of our days, we will be happy. But if we see only the things that irritate us, that make life difficult, we will suffer. By remembering to look at things positively, we can guarantee a happy future together. By focusing on the negative, we sign our relationship's death warrant.

Today, I see the glass and I describe it as half full.

SEPTEMBER 26

Apologizing

The famous line from the Love Story movie says that "love means never having to say you're sorry". Because ideal love always forgives? Or because we can't be wrong when we speak in the name of love? In any event, reality is something quite different from the movies. To live in a relationship, we must be ready and willing to apologize when we are wrong — which means that we will have to apologize on a fairly regular basis!

Every individual deserves to be treated with sensitivity and respect. When I share someone's intimacy, the chances of trampling their feelings are exacerbated. Sometimes a tone of voice, an oversight or a bad mood can be the straw that breaks the camel's back. At such times, we must be willing to apologize, if only to show the other person that we are sensitive and receptive to their needs and to demonstrate that their well-being and happiness are important to us.

Today, I agree to apologize when I have gone too far and when I have hurt my partner. By apologizing, I demonstrate that my partner's happiness is important to me.

September 27

Seeing What is Important

"We live in a upside-down world. What we think is important is often completely trivial in reality. We work hard at building sand castles. We rush to fill our lives with conquests and possessions but we are blind to the one true goal: freedom."

— Marc Alain

Today, I embrace the freedom to explore, to take risks, to be spontaneous and to do what I need to do. Today, I am ready to embrace my freedom because I know that I am responsible and aware. I know that I am able to live with the results and consequences of my new freedom. And I know that I will always be true and faithful to my inner being.

SEPTEMBER 28

Being Alone in a Relationship

"We were like two robots. Our life together was so well structured that we knew what we would be doing on Tuesday night of each week. Our relationship had become so predictable, I felt as if I were in a dream. But above all, I felt alone. In the morning I got up and went through the same motions, thinking the same thoughts. When we went out together, I felt no joy, no excitement. Somewhere along the way, we lost our sense of adventure and we sank into a mind-deadening routine that killed our love life."

— BEATRICE P.

We all know that we can be involved in a relationship and still feel alone. We wake up one fine day and we have the profound sense of being alone, of rehearsing a play whose ending we know by heart. Our relationship is no longer of any interest to us and we feel that we are drifting further and further away from the people and things around us. When this reality take roots, we need to react quickly to bring intensity, passion and adventure back into our lives and back into our relationship.

Today, I know that I am responsible for my happiness and the satisfaction I get from our relationship. If I feel alone or stuck in a monotonous routine, I do something to escape from my shell.

My Own Personal Clan

"I remember that when I was single, I felt left out and different from everybody else. Of course, I had friends and affairs, but I didn't feel as if I belonged anywhere. My relationship helped me find my place in the world. With Mary, I feel that I am part of a couple, a family. My relationship gives me the opportunity to play a role, to fulfill a mission and to take on life's many different situations. In our relationship, I feel that my identity is more stable and I feel that I have the support of someone else. I see my relationship as my own personal clan."

— LUCIANO W.

Today, I see that because of our relationship I am better prepared to take on the challenges of life. The stability of our couple gives me the support I need and it gives me the feeling that I am doing something that goes beyond myself and my own needs.

SEPTEMBER 30

Passion

Early in a relationship, we do things we don't dare to do as the years go by — for example, taking a bath together, making love in every room in the apartment and on every piece of furniture, walking hand in hand and writing love letters. We still love our partner, but our love has changed. Our love is more reasonable and less passionate. We go to bed together, but to sleep. We leave notes around the house, but to say that we'll be late for dinner. Deep down, we know that we're with the right person and that we love him or her completely, but our gestures and words have changed.

We should be careful not to wait until the other person heads for the door before fanning the flames of love and passion once again.

Today, I see that I can create moments of passion and tenderness. I can fan the flames of passionate love in our relationship.

OCTOBER 1

The Reward for Our Efforts

A relationship is a long-term undertaking. When the basis of the relationship is solid and when both partners are working towards the same objectives, their relationship deepens and matures over the years, with the tranquil presence of each other and the roles they play in each other's lives. A fundamental understanding brings us together, by virtue of which we no longer feel the need to question the trivial occurrences that make up day-to-day life. When a relationship is solid, we are content to live — it's as simple as that.

Unfortunately, our society of consumption overwhelms us with instant or throwaway products, and accustoms us to get what we want at the push of a button. And so we come to believe that happiness is an instant commodity as well and when we can't have exactly when we want, we begin to look somewhere else. As we turn elsewhere, we fail to give ourselves the time it takes to carry out the project we share with our partner. And time is of the essence in a relationship. In the early stages of life together, we must determine and understand the other's expectations and viewpoints. This takes time. When the adaptation period is over, we truly begin to enjoy the reward that comes with our mutual efforts.

Today, I know that a relationship requires long-term work and effort. I will be patient so that I can enjoy the reward of our efforts.

Taking the Time to be Together

There is no place else on earth where we are as loved and as valued as within a couple. Within a love relationship, each partner has an extremely privileged place. We can express ourselves freely and we can be with someone who accepts us as we are. Why try to escape a relationship for the sake of being independent? No where else on earth can we be as free and as self-reliant. Why dream of being with someone else when in our partner, we have everything we could possibly want?

The important thing is simply to take the time to be together. Take the time to listen, to speak and share.

Today, I have decided to take the time to live with and truly appreciate the role my partner fulfills in my life. I know that I can enjoy every experience in our relationship and I can live life to the fullest with my partner by my side.

Rewarding Effort

Every individual is unique and important. We can foster excellence in individuals by giving them our encouragement and by recognizing their efforts. We all try to do the best we can so that we can enjoy a good quality of life. In a relationship, we work together every day and this in itself is a reward. When we make the effort of combining our energy and our time to build a better life, there is also a reward. Life cannot revolve solely around work. We must be able to celebrate and encourage each other every day. When we tell our partners that we love and appreciate them, we are rewarding their efforts. When we take the time to pamper them at the end of the day, we are rewarding their efforts. When we bring them a small gift for no special reason, we are rewarding their efforts.

Today, I can recognize and reward the efforts we both make each day to build a strong and positive relationship. Another day spent together deserves to be noted and celebrated.

OCTOBER 4

Understanding Our Partner

I believe that when we truly listen, we can understand our partner. Each person chooses to understand or not to understand. We can agree or refuse to take the time to determine our partner's needs, intentions and motives. But understanding can make a world of difference. As soon as I understand my partner and he or she feels understood, the relationship is magically transformed. Most conflicts are caused by a refusal to try to understand the other person. One partner takes a stand and wants to be right at all costs.

Understanding is crucial to the harmony between two people. We must be capable of seeing the other person's point of view in all its aspects. If we resist, arguments and misunderstandings are inevitable. Understanding requires a certain level of good will and effort. We must want to understand the other person and we must give him or her the feeling that we do understand them.

Today, I see that understanding is a vital factor in a relationship. I can understand my partner's point of view without giving up my own. When I agree to be present and to listen to my partner, the relationship is magically transformed.

OCTOBER 5

Autumn Leaves

"When autumn comes, we stay at home more often. We like to build a fire in the fireplace, sip warm tea and watch the leaves fall. We feel that at last, we can spend some quiet time together. Time and life seem to have slowed and we have the chance to talk and laugh together. We take long walks and we play cards as we listen to classical music. Autumn is the ideal season to celebrate our relationship."

— MARY B.

A relationship finds its expression in simple gestures and words. We sometimes feel that the couple is a zone for negotiation between two complex human beings. But two people who love each other and who love to spend time together can slow down the pace and simply appreciate their relationship. In these instances, the couple fulfills its fundamental mission.

Today, I know that my relationship is a simple pleasure that I can appreciate at any time. I can simply be there and I can enjoy the time spent with my partner.

October 6

Celebrating the Exceptional

"What's exceptional about our relationship is that we're still alive, well and together after 30 years of marriage. Our life together hasn't always been easy. I threatened to leave on more than one occasion, but I always stayed because I wouldn't have been able to live with the sense of failure. I knew that I was in the right relationship with the right person, but it took me years before I could calm down and be content with where I was and where I was going. I felt that things weren't moving fast enough and that Emily wasn't being serious enough. What I hadn't understood was that there's no use tilting after windmills and running around aimless without a clear plan of action. As the years went by I became more mature and luckily, Emily had stuck by me in spite of my impulsive and impatient personality."

— Matt L.

There is always something exceptional about a relationship. We should look at our relationship and we should be aware that it is built on a love that is exceptional in itself. Two people agreeing to share their lives for better and for worse is exceptional. Overcoming our primary instincts and staying with a partner to build a relationship and to communicate our thoughts and feelings is exceptional.

Today, I celebrate the exceptional.

OCTOBER 7

In an Ideal World

In an ideal world, there would be no war and human beings of good will would live in peace. In an ideal world, we would find the help we needed and people would work together to build a better future for all children. In an ideal world, the love in a relationship would last for a lifetime and everyone would meet the partner who is ideal for them.

Although we don't live in an ideal world and day-to-day life for many is a battle for survival, we should never give up the idea of a better world. Each of us has a share in the collective responsibility. Each of us can choose to create hours of joy or hours of misery. Each of us can lend a hand and agree to help a neighbor in whatever way possible.

Today, I know that my attitude and my actions can change things. I can be loving or indifferent. I can create harmony in my relationships or I can create chaos. Today, I can contribute in my own way to creating a better world.

October 8

Stress

Modern life brings us many types of stress: family, relationship and professional responsibilities; inconveniences, noise, unexpected situations, conflicts and disappointments. Stress — the friction between what we want and what the environment offers us in response to our expectations — can have major consequences. Some people react better to stress than others. In an ideal context, a relationship allows us to relax and to rid ourselves of the day's stress. But we all know that a relationship can be a source of additional stress.

We must determine what is good and what is necessary. If a partner is undergoing enormous stress that surpasses his or her ability to adapt, we must be sufficiently sensitive not to add to it; on the contrary, we should do all that we possibly can to alleviate his or her stress. A relationship allows us to manage stress more efficiently. By being sensitive and by cooperating with each other, we can find solutions to life's demands and preoccupations.

Today, I help my partner. Instead of adding to his or her everyday stress, I look for ways to alleviate it so that I can restore the harmony in our relationship.

Dwelling on Thoughts

The end of a relationship takes place in our hearts. Often, conflicts and breakups occur in our minds before they are translated into reality. We think of comments that have been made. We forgive, but we don't forget. We think of all the unfairness we've suffered and we fuel a deep bitterness. The thoughts that inhabit us bring waves of emotion and we begin to see things in the relationship that aren't really there.

We must remember that thoughts are fleeting. They come and they go. A relationship is real. The thoughts that visit us are not necessarily real although they show us how we perceive the reality of our relationship.

Today, I refuse to dwell on negative thoughts. I let them come and go, but I pay no special attention to them. Instead, I concentrate on the outside world by communicating with my partner.

October 10

Whipped Cream

All of us need to know that we are loved and appreciated for what we are. In a relationship, we often take the good things for granted. But when we look elsewhere, we see that the good things are the result of our work and our dedication. We should recognize our partner's contribution to our life together. We should show our love and appreciation as often as we can. A tender gesture, a small comment that says: "You are wonderful" can make a big difference in a person's day.

Today, I take the time to compliment my partner. I see how my partner has changed my life and I tell him (or her) that I appreciate his efforts.

October 11

Playing Together

We can play together whether we're six or sixty. Playing isn't something exclusive to children. We can let go, play and laugh together. Many couples include play in their everyday lives. They play with the children or plan outings with friends to play parlor games or sports. When people get together to play, exchanges are fun and comments are lighthearted. To be happy, we should play together. Life is sufficiently serious and at times, even depressing. By playing, we can reduce stress and add excitement and vitality to our relationship.

Today, I want to include play in our relationship. There are many games we can play together. By playing together, we find the fun and wonderment of childhood.

October 12

The Health and Well-Being of the Couple

The couple is a sanctuary that protects us from illness and confusion. This sanctuary is our domain. In it, we are sheltered in the security of love and the protection that the couple offers. Together, we can heal. Together, we can work towards our happiness and our fulfillment. Modern life is filled with traps and misadventures. But the couple is an island of peace for those who are willing to share their lives. I will be there for you, no matter what. I will be there when you don't feel good, to bring you the relief and the tenderness you deserve. I will keep you close to me forever and I will give you all that your body and your heart desire.

Today, I know that the couple is my sanctuary. In our relationship, I am well and I am at peace. In my relationship, I find the health and the well-being I need.

October 13

Giving What We Would Like to Receive

The intimacy of the couple forces us to reveal even the smallest facet of ourselves. Eventually, our partner will see us act or react in various situations and at various emotional levels. Given the fact that we share an intimate space, we put our partner through several emotional phases. Despite the ups and downs inherent in life as part of a couple, we also nurture the desire to pamper and protect the other person. So how can we establish a balance between respecting our partner and the need to be ourselves and to express ourselves freely? The answer is to give what we would like to receive.

You know how you like people to treat you. You know what gestures of consideration touch you. You know what tone of voice you do not want people to take when they speak to you. So use your own parameters to determine how your loved one would like to be treated. You can weather an emotional storm without lashing out at your partner. Each person has a right to their emotions, but there is a proper way of expressing them. By expressing them appropriately, we can avoid serious disagreements.

Today, I give my partner what I would like to receive. I know that I can be myself and I can respect my partner at the same time.

October 14

It's Warm Inside

"What I like about our relationship is that we can both be ourselves under any circumstances. At work, I have to deal with all sorts of people and I have to handle the worst situations without showing any reaction. At home, I can let go and I can express myself freely. Michael loves me as I am. When I get home at night, I feel like I'm on vacation. We prepare the evening meal together and we look at a movie on TV. Or we walk the dog. Nothing complicated. We love being together."

— Agnes H.

Comfort and pleasure are invaluable for people who work under difficult circumstances. For them, the relationship is a haven of tranquility on a stormy sea. We can create a climate of relaxation and well-being within a relationship. Creating such a climate is easy if we agree on the fact that the relationship belongs to us and brings us the joy and comfort we need.

Today, I see that our relationship can be like a comfortable old pair of slippers. A relationship is not necessarily a work of introspection and constant questioning. It can offer a stable climate of warmth and security.

October 15

Family and Children

The couple gives rise to the family and the family gives rise to the community. The community gives rise to the nation and the nation gives rise to the world. At the root, there is us and there is our children. We all want to create a warm and safe climate for our children. We want to grow with them and to include them in our lives. Children are complete beings who need our love and our support. The family can be a place of joy, love and mutual help. Children grow up so fast and look to us and copy our attitudes and behaviors. We know that we have the responsibility of showing them how to become good citizens, how to love and how to succeed in life. By creating a loving and harmonious couple, we teach them the most important of all lessons.

Today, I see that our relationship can serve as a model. My attitudes and my behaviors influence all members of the family. By being fair and tolerant, by behaving lovingly and politely towards my partner, I accomplish a very important mission.

OCTOBER 16

Saying "I Love You"

We sometimes forget that three little words can make all the difference in our partner's day. Said thoughtfully, *I love you* can change a mood and gives wings to a heart.

Today, I take the time to say "I love you" to my partner.

Forgiving

A couple cannot survive without genuine forgiveness. We are beings on a journey of growth and discovery. We all have limitations, barriers and aberrations. All of us must make our own mistakes and bear the consequences of our failings. A relationship can help us recover our equilibrium after we have erred. Within a relationship, each partner must have the ability to forgive, as each partner must be willing to forget.

Today, I see how forgiveness can be a precious tool in our relationship's development. I am human and I am living with someone who has his or her own limitations. I can forgive myself and I can forgive my partner because I know that each day, we try to improve and to strengthen the bonds between us.

October 18

Sex Before Marriage

"I believe that sex before marriage has killed the couple. In our day, we feel we should test the merchandise before buying it. So we can have our cake without making any commitment. People are content with short-term gratification until such time as they realize that they are growing old alone. At at the age of 35 or 40, they decide that they are ready for commitment. These behavior patterns weaken the couple, marriage and the family. We don't necessarily want to start a family at age 40. Somewhere along the way, we've lost our family values. We lost the true and profound sense of long-term commitment."

— Richard M.

In the past 30 years, we've seen the breakup of the family unit and the traditional couple. Now we see a variety of formulas such as single-parent families, committed singles, common-law relationships, casual relationships, etc. Are individuals freer today? They are free to experience all kinds of affairs, to live together, to separate and to live alone. Everywhere, we see the fragments and vestiges of the couple and the family. Committed couples have become almost a minority. Yet the couple and the family are the foundation on which the world rests.

Today, I know that strength and stability lies in commitment. Despite the lack of support and role models in society, I will create an alliance based on love.

OCTOBER 19

The Limits of the Human Body

Everyone knows that the human body has its limitations. But the soul is limitless. It is communicative and powerful beyond our imagination. We look at someone and we see a body. However, the body is unimportant because it is bound to age and to disappear. Beyond the body, there is a timeless soul. When we become part of a couple, often we are attracted by a body and by physical beauty, but soon we connect with the spiritual being that animates that body. A relationship can last a lifetime and well beyond, provided we want it to last. We have known each other for a very long time. And suddenly, we have the opportunity of living together in this incarnation.

Today, I know that the soul is timeless and that the love I give in this life will belong to me forever. I can create links of friendship that will last an eternity. I can love well beyond the limits of my physical body. Why be contented with so little when I know that I can love the soul and give my body and soul to my loved one?

October 20

Knowing When to Stop

"She never knew when to stop. I'd be tired when I got home after work and I had to listen to her complaining and whining until we went to bed. When she'd start I'd turn off a switch in my head and she'd fade into the background, like any other noise. When I couldn't take it any more I'd put on my coat and I'd go out. She'd get even more frantic when I'd leave, but I just couldn't listen to her when she started in. She could go on and on for hours, even days. On the pretext that we were involved in a relationship, she thought that she could say anything that came into her mind, that she could preach at me for as long as she wanted. I just couldn't stand her behavior."

— Peter P.

Communication is a two-way street. We say something and we wait for a response. After we've heard and understood the response, we may want to add something else. Often, the communication hasn't been effective. No one wants to hear. There is a fundamental breakdown in the communication process. To make our relationship a success and to live in harmony, our communication must be honest and ongoing. We must react quickly to any breakdown in communication within a relationship. Our happiness and our survival depends on good communication.

Today, I see that the vitality of our relationship lies in our will and aptitude to communicate.

October 21

Where Are all the Prince Charmings?

"Like all girls, I thought that I'd meet my Prince Charming. And when I met my knight in shining armor, my life would be changed as if by magic. We would get married and live happily ever after. But like most women, I kissed a lot of frogs before I found my Prince Charming. And my prince started to be a lot less charming after a few months of married life. We should teach children that life is hard and that with a bit of luck, they might find a bit of happiness in a relationship. This way nobody would be disappointed when they grew up."

— Lauren R.-M.

It's hard to overcome the ideas we have on the ideal couple. We entertain preconceived ideas on love relationships. A relationship is a road travelled by two people. It includes disappointments, difficulties and the need for adjustments along the way. But cooperation between partners brings joy and rewards. More wonderful than any myth, the reality of a love relationship is a process of growth that leads us to self-discovery and to the discovery of our partner's inner being.

Today, I can set aside my mistaken ideas on relationships and I can focus on the reality of our relationship. By looking at and appreciating reality as it is, I can live life with my partner to the fullest, in the present moment.

October 22

The Fear of Loneliness

If our main reason for starting a relationship is to avoid being alone, the motivation will never be enough to ensure its survival. Loneliness can be extremely painful and it is not a goal in itself, except for individuals aspiring to the higher levels of monastic reclusion. We are rarely alone by choice. But if we must be alone, we can look at the experience positively with the knowledge that it is a time to clarify our expectations and our objectives in life. We can also consider the start of a new relationship with the knowledge that we have taken the time we needed to truly learn to know and value ourselves.

Today, I no longer try to run from loneliness. I embrace it because I know that by living my loneliness to the fullest, I will find my true self. And when I am ready for a new relationship, I will have lived through the experiences I need to fully appreciate this new turn of events in my life.

OCTOBER 23

Family Tragedies

When we begin a relationship, we enter the overall reality of an extended family. Our partner brings a family and a family history to the relationship and we bring ours. This fusion of different experiences and different realities creates a specific and special context: expectations, family rituals, shared attitudes and family responsibilities. With an extended family comes the potential of being exposed to family tragedies. Tragedies (illnesses, dependencies, violence, death) can affect a relationship. We are always free to choose our attitude to the tragedies that can affect our own family or our partner's family. The important thing is to avoid becoming embroiled in such tragedies and to protect the relationship from their potentially devastating effects.

Today, I see that our relationship exposes us to the reality of two extended families. I watch the events that occur and while being cordial and sympathetic to the members of our respective families, I avoid becoming involved in the family tragedies that happen around us.

October 24

My Own Reality

I have my own reality and you have yours. We are involved in a relationship and as a couple, we have a reality that goes beyond our individual realities. I will not ask you to abandon your own reality or to subordinate it for the benefit of our reality as a couple. I ask that you respect my reality and that you be aware of our shared reality. If you share your reality with me, I will try to understand and to see things from your point of view. If your reality is based on the negation of my reality or our shared reality, I ask that you revise your point of view and that you make the necessary changes to your outlook. If my reality does not reflect our shared reality, I am prepared to make the necessary adjustments. By communicating, we can solve any problem that we may encounter.

Today, I know that you have your reality and that I have mine. Our reality as a couple must be the genesis of our two realities.

October 25

Taming the Wind

The human body is driven by a vital force. This vital momentum, the human mind, is present in a relationship. In a relationship, two minds join to form a material and spiritual alliance. The couple has a dynamic life and a direction given to it by the synthesis of our dreams, of our aspirations and of our desires as spiritual beings. The couple helps us tame and orient the vital momentum of the spirit that manifests itself in love, sharing and common projects. The couple cannot remain in a static form. It changes and evolves with the growing awareness of the two partners who comprise it. In a couple, I participate in the evolution of a living entity that is greater than me alone. I live in the consciousness and identity of love and learning.

Today, I know that I live in the consciousness and identity of love and learning. I grow each day within our couple and I am increasingly closer to the fundamental nature of love.

October 26

Do It Now

"Time passes quickly and life is so short! The person you love and you will not be here on earth forever. As long as we are here, as long as we are human beings who love each other, we must speak kind words, have fun, do things together, exchange gifts, open our hearts and console one another. Time is not eternal. Regardless of what you planned to accomplish, do it now."

— Daphne Rose Kingma

Today, I know that there is no need to wait to express the most beautiful things I feel, all the love I have within me.

All Our Memories

"I feel as if the years have slipped through my fingers like so many grains of sand. I sit down with Steve and we look at pictures of our wedding, our life together, our children and the people we've known over the years. All sorts of emotions come flooding back to me. I can even smell the smells and taste the tastes as if I were actually experiencing the things I see on the photographs. Steve always has a story to tell, an event that marked him and that he may have shared with me already. These moments are precious because they show us how rich and full our life has been. We spent so many wonderful years together and now, in the twilight years of our relationship, we still have love."

— LAURA G.

No one can take our memories from us. As our relationship evolves, we accumulate shared memories. These shared memories are proof of the richness and depth of our love. Our lives have changed over the years but our relationship has withstood the test of time. We can be happy together and we can be proud of ourselves.

Today, I see that we have many happy memories. Our memories warm our hearts and strengthen our relationship.

OCTOBER 28

Living Simply in a Complex World

A relationship need not be complex. We can live together, love each other and make each other happy without looking for the deep meaning behind things. Many couples struggles with an endless process of introspection that leads nowhere. They are convinced that there is a profound and vague malaise hidden in the depths of their relationship. They torment themselves, ask themselves questions and forget to live day by day with what life has given them. A relationship can be a simple and comforting experience that allows each partner to breathe in large breaths of refreshing, revitalizing air.

We can play, laugh, make love and sleep without questioning the relationship. We can enjoy the material wealth we have while working towards a more ideal situation. A relationship should be lived minute by minute. If we spend all our time questioning, we will create a climate of total and absolute confusion.

Today, I see that our relationship as something simple. By being present in the here and now, I can enjoy the positive relationship I have created with my partner.

October 29

Just a Gigolo!

Monogamy has taken a beating in recent decades. We are quick to accept unfaithfulness and divorce, as if marriage and a stable relationship were secondary considerations. What we consider important today is professional success, careers and material wealth. If a man amasses a fortune and achieves social prestige and if he wants to take a mistress, no one thinks twice. We have become a society of gigolos. Faithfulness, commitment, loyalty and other noble values have been displaced by economic realities. The human being has fallen into total confusion.

However, there is a difference between these people and those who have chosen to live a life based on a moral code and sound values. In general, the latter group is happier. Their children and their families are the center of their lives and they are more successful. The contrast between the two groups clearly demonstrates that the lack of a code of conduct leads to confusion and emotional unbalance.

Today, I recognize the power of a code of conduct based on sound values. I apply my code in all aspects of my life and I enjoy the rewards of a life of integrity.

October 30

Happier Together

"When I assess the situation, I see that I'm happier in a relationship than alone. At times I've wanted to end things so that I could be on my own. I'd be free and I could do whatever I wanted to do. But when I think of it, life in a relationship is much richer and much more interesting. I have the profound feeling of belonging to something and having a specific role to play in life. If I was alone, I'd want to be in a relationship because I like the stability and the pleasures of living as part of a couple. I see that life is better when I'm in a relationship."

— John F.

Today, I see that our relationship offers me all that I need to be happy. In hard times, I sometimes think that I would be happier if I were single. However, single life is much too limited to fill my needs.

OCTOBER 31

Being or Having

"Possessions can never do for us what people can. Things, regardless of how impressive, can never satisfy us deep in our hearts. We need to survive and we need to be loved. Material objects can distract us for awhile but will not fill the void we feel inside when we are not loved. Most would part with all their riches to find true and lasting love. Some may think that by accumulating wealth they will attain power and security, but in their heart of hearts they know that being loved will always be more powerful and gratifying then having things."

— CAROL SMITH

Today, I recognize that a relationship is an experience, not a possession. We like to accumulate things, but a relationship is something that is, it is not something that we have. I can never possess my partner, but I can live and choose freely to be with him or her. Possessions are fleeting. The experience of our relationship and the presence of my partner are lasting.

NOVEMBER 1

Opening the Door to Love

"I spent years before I realized that it was impossible for anyone to have a relationship with me. Deep down, I didn't want to come into any real contact with anyone, I didn't want anyone to get to know me. I didn't want to be vulnerable or to feel trapped. I think that what people saw in me was a kind of detachment or arrogance. My relationships couldn't last because the women who came into my life felt that I was indifferent. My defence mecanism lasted years, until such time as I realized I had not one friend, not one person I loved. I was dying of boredom and loneliness. So I put away my shield and my armor and I let others come into my life."

— MICHAEL R.

If we want a relationship, we have to be accessible. If we live our lifes as if we were watching a film, without making any real investment, or if we build impenetrable walls around us, we will never know the joy of love and intimacy. Vulnerability, exchange and authentic communication involve a certain degree of danger. When I am reachable, I can be hurt. But without the creative experience of love and friendship, life has no meaning.

Today, I open the door to love and I am available to other people. Of course, I run the risk of being hurt, but I also run the risk of living a valuable experience and undergoing a profound change thanks to our relationship.

November 2

Finding Someone to Love

We hear all kinds of magic formulas for love and relationships. Some say we should find someone who loves us more than we love them. Others claim that a relationship is a sharing of love: we must love the other person as much as they love us. If one person loves the other too much, because of an inability to be objective about the relationship, he or she risks being exploited. All these magic formulas are just that: formulas. They are vague ideas that have no basis in the objective reality of a relationship. We cannot measure the level of love that exists in a relationship and each person experiences a relationship in his or her own way.

One thing is sure: to take part in a living and passionate relationship, we must feel loved and we must know that we genuinely love in return. When these elements are in place, relationships can grow. Feeling that we love more or less than the other person loves us will bring us very little, unless we are seeking a strategic advantage. A relationship is neither a war nor a commercial strategy.

Today, I feel that all of the elements are in place to make our relationship a success. I know that there is enough love between us to keep us together and to give us the will we need to continue to share our lives.

November 3

Conquests

"When I was in college, my friends and I had a little contest that we used to call climing Mount Everest. The contest consists of seeing who could sleep with the most girls during the year, with proof (as proof, we had to bring back something very personal, like underwear). I had just begun searching for candidates when I met Jane. I immediately realized that I couldn't just seduce her and drop her. Jane was no idiot. She let me get close, but she wouldn't go all the way. After a few dates I started to like her a lot and I dropped out of the contest. Why lose my time with silly, superficial contact when I could deepen a relationship and experience something truly significant?"

— Karl L.

Sexual relations are a form of short-term gratification. A relationship brings us a world of experiences and satisfaction. When we are young, we want to prove that we can be seductive and charming. With maturity, we want to prove that we can build something more significant and more lasting.

Today, I want to be close to my partner and I want to experience our relationship to the fullest. Our relationship brings me all I need and more. Why would I want to jeopardize it?

The Art of Consoling

A relationship requires that we be present and that we understand our partner. We have to see life through our partner's eyes and we have to identify with our partner and his or her aspiratons, motivatons, fears and disappointments. We need not be sad to understand and appreciate the other person's sadness. We need not suffer to understand and support a partner in his or her suffering. By holding a hand and by saying: "I am here to share your joy and your suffering", I have gone at least half way in consoling the one I love.

Today, I make a commitment to be there for my partner, in joy and in hardship. I am the shoulder that provides support. I am the extended hand. I am the ladder.

November 5

Love Heals

Love is a state of mind and a feeling. But love is also a force that transforms and heals. In life, we can be confronted with many different experiences. Some can be particularly painful and can leave their mark forever. Fortunately, love can console us and heal us. Love penetrates our depths and finds our essence. When we are with someone we love, someone who wants our well-being, his or her love permeates us, soothes us and heals the wounds of the past. Affinity, love and admiration are harmonic waves that eliminate all confusion and all pain.

Today, I use the curing power of love to soothe my partner's pain. When we feel the power of love in our lives, we can overcome all forms of distress.

November 6

The Value of Integrity

We all know when we are being honest, and when we are being dishonest. We all know when we are telling the truth, and when we are hiding it. We all know when we are making the decision that is in the best interest of our relationship, and when we are making the decision that is the easiest to make. We can go to the heart of a relationship when we are capable of being faithful to ourselves, to our principles and to the truths we know in our inner self. The small transgressions we are responsible for, the small lies and the half-truths we use to protect ourselves eventually destroy our relationships. By being honest every day and under all circumstances, we can live happily and we can enjoy and experience our love relationship to the fullest.

Today, I live with an open heart. I am faithful to my principles and to the truths I know. I know that my relationship can grow if I am honest at all times.

November 7

Cohabitaton

"I was in a small café with four of my girlfriends. We were all involved in relationships. In the group, I was the only one who was married. My girlfriends asked me why I had gotten married when I could have moved in with my boyfriend instead. According to them, marriage was something superfulous and it could hurt each partner's sense of independance and self-reliance. I answered that in my eyes, marriage is an official commitment that two people freely consent to make. Peter was willing to make a commitment to protect and support me for the rest of our lives. I think that women always lose when they move in with their boyfriends."

— Christine V.

More and more people think that there are more advantages to common-law relationships than to marriage. They believe that even when children are involved, common-law relationships are more modern and cool. But the institution of marriage has a number of advantages over common-law relationship because it makes the union official and protects both parties. However, marriage is not a guarantee of a lifetime relationship and it can end in divorce and financial consequences that lead both parties to reflect on the situation before putting an end to their agreement.

Today, I know that I have the choice between cohabitation and marriage.

NOVEMBER 8

Free to Invent

Today, I know that we are free to invent the relationship we want. Why try to imitate and comply with stereotypes not truly suited to us, when we can invent a relationship that resembles us and that lets us be who we really are?

Today, I want to be myself and I appreciate the person I am.

NOVEMBER 9

Life on a Tightrope

No one can live on a tightrope, knowing that the least false step can cost them their lives. A relationship allows each person to live and express themselves freely. However, many people live in fear. They are convinced that if they express themselves freely or if they choose to do something on their own initiative, they will be scolded and rejected. This type of relationship is not a relationship of love between two partners, it is a relationship of master-slave subservience.

Today, I refuse to live on a tightrope. I must have the opportunity to express myself and to live freely under all circumstances. If I see that my partner is seeking to restrict my freedom, I rectify the situation. A relationship must be based on freedom of choice and expression.

NOVEMBER 10

Fatal Strategy

"My sister always tends to end up with men who like to make her suffer. When I met her latest boyfriend, I wondered what she could possibly have seen in him. He had no manners, he was unemployed and he had no prospects for the future. Sometimes, I think she likes to suffer. She'll stay with him for a year or two, she'll have wasted her time and she'll be mistreated. Then, when the relationship is over, she'll spend her time crying her eyes out until she finds another man who'll make her suffer every bit as much."

— MONICA L.

We all know someone whose relationships are like a Greek tragedy. Everyone around them knows well in advance that the relationship won't last, that it is based on the fear of loneliness and on suffering. No one can intervene but eventually, things turn out exactly as predicted. The people who find themselves in this type of relationship time and time again are prisoners of their own fatal strategy. They do nothing to build a healthy relationship; they look for jailers so that they can play victim.

Today, I see that each of us must live through our own experiences and draw our own conclusions. I cannot protect people from the fatal strategies that bring them into unhealthy relationships. I can only be there if they want my help and my advice when they are prepared to change.

November 11

Words That Make All the Difference

Today, I can say the words that make all the difference. I love you. You are important to me. I am doing this or that because I love you. You are the most important person in my life. Without you, life would have no meaning. I will be with you forever. You are simply wonderful. I am so happy I met you. I am so happy to be with you. You have changed my life forever. I love you more today than when we first met. I am happy to grow old with you. You are the only person I have ever been truly in love with.

Today, I want to express my love to you because you are important to me.

Anniversaries

Relationship anniversaries and wedding anniversaries are important. They are an opportunity to pay tribute to our relationship and to celebrate our love. The fact that we have been together for one year, five years or 20 years proves that our relationship can withstand the test of time and that it is still alive and healthy. We look at the road we've travelled together and we see that there are still things to discover and celebrate. We are happy to have chosen to live together and to have chosen to stay together.

Today, we celebrate our relationship and we remember why we chose to live together and to stay together. Our relationship is a source of love and joy. Why not take the time to celebrate the love that brings us so much pleasure and warmth?

NOVEMBER 13

The Enemies of Self-Esteem

Self-esteem — the positive perception that each of us entertains with regard to ourselves — is vital to a good relationship. Some behaviors nurture self-esteem and others harm it. We know that denigrating comments, drug addiction, dependence on gambling or alcohol or the lack of objectives in life can hinder our ability to love and to succeed. If we want to grow together, we must drive away the enemies of self-esteem when they appear. Our well-being and the survival of our relationship depends on it. The enemies of self-esteem filter into our lives in sly and seeminlgy insignificant ways. We fail to see the problem until it is too late. For this reason, we must always be extremely vigilant and when we see warning signs, we must react immediatly to eliminate what can potentially sabotage our well-being and our survival.

Today, I am vigilant and attentive to the behaviors that can harm my self-esteem and my partner's self-esteem. I refuse the things that can hurt my self-esteem because my relationship is important to me and I want to live in peace and harmony every day of my life.

November 14

Stupidity

"I look around me and I see that the biggest problem we face is the human being's stupidity. People endlessly repeat the same blunders and they learn nothing from their mistakes. They judge situations poorly and show the kind of behavior that jeopardizes their own survival. We see intelligent people do the stupidest things in the name of pride or because they lack the courage to see things as they really are. They judge people by their appearance and cast a superficial glance on the people around them and the experience life brings them. They don't realize that every person has value and that life is a precious experience that we can't afford to waste."

— Gregory C.

No one can save you from yourself. No one can make you happy and help you live a positive life. No one can force you to use your intelligence and your resources fairly and rationally. You are the master of your own destiny and everything you experience in life is the result of your attitudes and your actions. No one can save you from your own stupidity if you choose to live without any thought to the consequences of your actions.

Today, I see that I am the only person who is responsible for my situation. I can succeed and be happy by using my intelligence and my resources appropriately. If I experience hard times, I ask myself what I did to get myself into that situation.

November 15

A Woman's Place

Anthropology, the study of ancient cultures, tells us that in most native tribes, women were considered as possessions that could be traded. Women were distributed by the tribe's elders. The elders controlled the trade in women. With the trade in women came power and the control over all the material goods circulating within the tribe. A man was not given a woman without good reason. He was given a woman because of his family links and the possessions his family had to trade.

The modern relationship is based on the principle of free trade between equal partners. But some men have the vestiges of the rites of trade from the past. Some still consider a woman to be a possession and not a free and equal human being. Without the recognition of our freedom and our equality, a relationship can never reach its full potential. Today's couple must be composed of two conscious and free beings.

Today, I see that a relationship cannot be based on the woman's subservience in relation to the man. The couple is an endeavor undertaken by two equal and responsible human beings.

NOVEMBER 16

Romantic Dinners

Romance is the honey in a relationship. When we take the time to dine by candlelight together and to speak the words of love softly and gently, we fan the flames of passion and we reinforce our love. Tenderness nourishes and calms the spirit, it focuses our awareness on the pleasure of being with the one we love.

Today, I prepare a romantic dinner. I am happy to spend a few tender and loving moments with my partner, simply to look into each other's eyes and hear each other's voice.

The Winter of Love

A relationship cannot accommodate winter. When we are together for practical reasons and when the magic has disappeared into the cold and the snow, the heart still beats — but the sun is so far away that love is hidden and tenderness is in the dark. How can we melt the frost that numbs the spirit of love? How can we rekindle our love when it is covered with a blanket of snow, making us feel it never existed? The answer is to take the first step, to extend a hand and to say "I would like to try again".

Today, I know that love can come back to life. Winter never lasts forever. The flowers of love can bloom under the warm sun of those who are willing to give themselves a second chance.

The Basis of a Happy Life

"I'm a simple man. I haven't got much of an education and I've had to work hard all my life. I worked to earn my living and to take care of my wife and children. Life isn't easy for a man from an ordinary background who has to work every day to feed his family. I've never had the chance to go on a vacation down South or to spend weekends polishing my Cadillac. Still, I feel rich. I have a wife who loves me and our family is close. And I feel that I did my share for society by working hard and by doing my job well."

— ARNOLD S.

The couple and the family are the basis of a happy life. In our consumer-based society, we sometimes forget what is most important. By being a good husband or wife, a good father or mother, a good worker, I can be proud and I am worthy of respect.

Today, I look around and I see that I have accomplished something. I may not be a movie star or a high powered CEO. But I am a person who lives according to my values and I contribute to the well-being of others.

Being Patient

A relationship calls for patience. Things may not always go as fast as we want them to, or in the direction we want them to take. But if the relationship is solid, with time we will reach our objectives. I am a human being and I have my strengths and my weaknesses. My partner is a human being with strengths and weaknesses. We can manage together and we can make the most of every situation. Patience can help us accept the inconveniences and problems that we encounter in our relationship.

Today, I see that our relationship is solid and strong. By being patient, I have every chance of being successful and enjoying a life of harmony, one day at a time.

Love, One Day at a Time

When we consider the possibility of making a commitment for life, the thought may seem overwhelming. We wonder if we have enough endurance and courage to keep the commitment, even for only a few years. We may also fear that the relationship will lose its vitality as time goes by. But if we decide to share our lives, one day at a time, the task suddenly becomes much more feasible. In short, we can live only one day at a time. We live minute by minute. And the minutes accumulate to make up an hour, a day, a year and finally, a lifetime. When we will be older, we will see that life has gone by quickly and that the choices we made when we were younger have made significant differences on our life as a whole.

Today, I look at our relationship one day at a time. By living in the present, I can enjoy life to the fullest.

November 21

Each Day is a New Beginning

Today, I know that each day is a new beginning. Yesterday we may have argued or we may have suffered a failure, but the dawn of a new day is here and it brings endless possibilities. We have learned from our past mistakes and we will continue to learn. Our love is not perfect, but we can improve it every day. Why should we cling to the past when before us we have a glorious future that we can build together, beginning today?

Today, I am open to all possibilities.

November 22

What I Can Change

There are things I can change and other things that I must accept. In my relationship, I must be capable of seeing what can be improved and what I can change. If I stubbornly try to change something about my partner that he or she does not want to change, I will make us both unhappy. But when I see something that can harm our relationship and I want to change it, then I must.

Today, I change what it is possible to change, I accept what I cannot change and I ask God for the wisdom to know the difference.

November 23

The Winning Number

Some people think that finding a partner is like playing the lottery. We need luck to meet the person for us but the chances of meeting the ideal person are so slim that we have to be content with someone who doesn't quite meet our expectations. In reality, we can attract exactly the person we want. There is no need to dream and hope to meet the ideal partner only to settle into a relationship that doesn't meet our criteria. We must adopt an attitude that leaves no room for even the possibility of failure. Knowing from the outset that we will meet the ideal person and being convinced that we deserve the best possible relationship, prepares us mentally and emotionally to exactly this eventuality. Based on a certainty, this mental attitude sends a powerful and clear message to the universe.

Today, I know that I need not be satisfied with a relationship that does not reflect my expectations and my desires. I have decided that I will not compromise in this regard and deep inside, I will maintain a winning attitude.

November 24

I See I've Changed

A relationship is a force for transformation in our lives. We cannot be involved in a relationship without undergoing change. A relationship calls for constant adjustments, it leads us to new and very powerful awareness, it requires that we be open to the other person and to the need for change. Inflexibility has no place in a couple because a couple is something in movement, like a dance. We must be flexible and we must move in unison to the music of our relationship.

Today, I see that I have changed. Our relationship has changed my life. Love is the most powerful motivation for positive change. I use our relationship to bring positive change to my life.

November 25

The Ability to Love

Love is not complex, but it requires a complex effort. We choose to love or not to love. When we choose to love for better or worse, we must devote every effort to maintaining our love and to making it grow. The conditions of our lives, the needs and demands of our partner and our own criteria for satisfaction all come into consideration in each of the choices we make daily. A relationship requires constant adjustments. We must be present and we must listen actively in all situations, to take from life the food we need to nourish our love. There can be no doubt that love appears spontaneously in our hearts, but the energy of love can fade quickly. Our efforts and the quality of those efforts can ensure that our love survives.

Today, I choose the labor of love that is our relationship.

November 26

Taking Care of Your Partner

To make a relationship successful, we must be interested in our partners and we must care for them. Everything we do for our partner strengthens the relationship. Some relationships come to an end because one person is more concerned with his or her own well-being than with the other person's well-being. At times we focus on our own well-being and our own happiness and the well-being and happiness of our partners seem to be an abstract and secondary consideration. If two partners are interested in each other and if they take care of each other, both will feel fulfilled and loved every single day. Why end a relationship when we are happy and when our needs are filled? A relationship is a little bit of heaven on earth when we focus our energy on satisfying the other person's needs and when the other person is as intensely involved in the satisfaction of our needs. Such is the nature of true sharing! Such is the magic of the couple as it manifests itself in every action, every thought and every word!

Today, I see that our relationship does not exist to satisfy my needs alone. I must be interested in my partner and I must take care of him or her every day. When I do, I create a climate of love and sharing that strengthens my relationship.

NOVEMBER 27

Making the Ordinary Extraordinary

"My boyfriend has the gift of changing life's very ordinary situations into opportunities to laugh and have fun. I had to go to the license bureau to pass a driving test. You can imagine how nervous I was about taking the test. Bill decided to take that afternoon off to come with me and encourage me. All the way to the license bureau he kept telling me what a good driver I was and how I would pass the test with flying colors. He described the trips to the country we could take together. He described the beautiful car we would buy and most of all, he made me laugh and relax. I passed the test without a hitch and Bill was waiting for me at the door — with balloons and confetti! I was really very happy. That man has a way of making life fun!"

— MARIANNA D.

Today, I see that I can transform life's ordinary situations. A relationship is not a job, but a climate that leads to joy and celebration. I can surprise my partner. I can organize small, unexpected celebrations. I can use my imaginaton to transform situations.

Relaxing Together

Today, I appreciate the relaxing times we spend together. I like the time we spend together housecleaning, talking, looking at a good movie on TV. I see that these relaxing times refresh us and bring us closer. I'm happy to see that even though most things in life go at a very fast pace, we can slow down the rhythm of things and truly enjoy our times together.

Today, I know how to enjoy a few minutes of relaxation with my partner.

Practising a Sport

We all know that fitness is an essential part of good health. Exercise and sports can also strengthen my relationship. We can practise sports together. There are many sports for two: tennis, badminton, cycling, mountain climbing, canoeing, walking — the list is virtually endless. Sports can revitalize and energize a relationship.

Today, I organize sports activities that we can do together. I see that sports can bring us closer, while keeping us young and healthy. Many sports can be played by two people. There are at least one or two sports that we would both like. We could even go out for a walk together in the evening.

November 30

Raising Children

Educating and socializing children is part of the reality of the couple. Children are the undertaking of a lifetime. From the day they are born, they need our love and attention. Much later, they leave to lead their own lives. They leave with the lessons they have learned at our side and with the love and encouragement we have given them during their formative years. Educating and socializing children is a beautiful shared project. The project can be carried out in an atmosphere of harmony, cooperation and wonderment. It can also take place in a climate of conflict and misery. If a couple is strong and united, the project will be all the less difficult and all the more successful.

Today, I welcome children in our relationship. I see that socializing our children will require a great deal of energy, love and patience. Our relationship is crucial because we must form a solid and happy couple to raise happy children. Children come into a relationship and eventually, they leave. Our life together will last a lifetime.

DECEMBER 1

Lack of Communication

Everyone agrees that communication is vital to a love relationship, and human relationships in general, and that the lack of communication can destroy a couple. Each partner must feel understood within the relationship. Each partner must show an interest in the other person and his or her concerns. Communication is simply the exchange of words or information. It is also the ability to listen and to understand the essential data that the other person chooses to communicate and it is our ability to have our partner listen to us and understand us. Communication is an active process that requires our attention and our presence. By being present, open and receptive, we can take part in a communication process and react to the imminent needs that are felt on a daily basis.

Today, I participate actively in our relationship by communicating with my partner. Communication is more than an exchange of words, it is the attention and intention I bring to our relationship.

DECEMBER 2

Say it with Flowers!

Everyone likes to get flowers. When we've been in a relationship for some time, we can forget that this simple gesture can transform our partner's day. Although simple, the gesture says "I love you and I'm thinking about you". Women can give flowers to their husbands. And men should always remember to give flowers to their wives. Flowers are the symbol of life and love and they can be given for no special reason and under all circumstances. Say it with flowers!

Today, I will bring a lovely bouquet of flowers to my partner to say: "I love you and I am with you today and forever. Of all the flowers on earth, you are the most beautiful."

DECEMBER 3

The Surprise Effect

Today, I decided to surprise my partner. I can go to her office at noon with a bouquet of flowers. I can announce that we're going out tonight and I make reservations at a new restaurant. I can write a poem in her honor and I can give it to her at just the right moment. I can repair the dishwasher that hasn't been working properly for a few days. I can bring the children to my parents next weekend so that we can have some time alone. There's no limit to what I can do to add a bit of excitement to our relationship. I see that the surprise effect can revitalize our relationship because it brings us together spontaneously.

Today, I've decided to surprise my partner.

Inlaws

People often criticize and make snide remarks about their inlaws. We often hear the cliche that inlaws are possessive, demanding and all too present in their daughters' or sons' relationships. They have to be kept at arm's length if you want to be happy. But don't forget that without your inlaws, you wouldn't have your partner. In part, your relationship is the result of their love and their efforts. Our inlaws deserve our love and our respect. They are sensitive human beings who want to love us and help us. They have our best interests at heart.

Today, I pay tribute to my inlaws. I see how they have contributed to my life by giving birth and raising my partner in a loving home.

DECEMBER 5

A Bit of Encouragement!

Words and gestures of encouragement are very important. We know that life can sometimes demand all of our efforts and all of our energy. When we receive unconditional support from a partner, we are more likely to succeed and to overcome life's obstacles. Encouraging a loved one usually takes very little time and energy. All we have to say is: I believe in you; I know that you can do this; you have all the talent it takes to be successful. We can lend our support with small, encouraging gestures: for example, preparing a good meal; doing the chores usually done by our partner so that he or she has more time for other things; making useful contacts or trying to come up with new solutions to the problems of the hour.

Today, I encourage my partner. I know that encouraging words and gestures can make all the difference in his or her day. It is as easy to encourage someone as it is to criticize them, but the end result is very different.

December 6

Saying Thank-You!

Saying thank-you shows that we are aware and that we appreciate the efforts our partners makes to help us and to make us happy. Because we are used to receiving things from our partner, we may forget to say thank-you. But no one likes to feel that they are part of the furniture. Each gesture is important. Each small thing that a loved one does to help us or to make us happy deserves to be thanked. Thank-you translates the fundamental recognition that should prevail between two people who share their lives.

Today, I take the time to say thank-you. When I see my partner's efforts to make our relationship happier and healthier, I say "Thank you!".

December 7

Indifference Kills

"I wasn't convinced that he still loved me. We were together physically, but I felt that there was no energy, no dynamics between us. We never argued. There was no major conflict between us. But I could feel his indifference. I felt that our relationship could go on or could come to an end and he wouldn't care either way. So I decided to make things happen. I couldn't accept his nonchalance based on routine and indifference. After many discussions, I told him that I wanted to end our relationship. He never understood why. But most of all, he never wanted to understand that a relationship isn't an airtight box. A relationship is a process of growth based on passion and mutual discovery."

— Andrea B.

John Lennon said: "As long as there is life, there is hope." Living beings cannot live in a climate of indifference. Living beings must enter into relationships with other living beings. Being alive means being present, involved, passionate and active. If you love someone, let them know that they are important to you. Live each minute with interest and desire. Life is not something you watch on television or you read about in a novel. Life deserves to be lived with intensity and passion.

Today, I am aware and present. I know that a set routine can feel safe, but to survive, a relationship also needs excitement and passion.

DECEMBER 8

Create, Create, Create!

A relationship is an ongoing project of creation. We create a relationship, then we create a relationship, and later we create a relationship. In a couple, nothing can be taken for granted. In the morning we should wake up with the intention of participating, giving, inventing our relationship, each day, until the end.

When we stop inventing our relationship, it begins to deteriorate. We must generate new experiences, formulate shared projects, and do new activities together if we want to maintain the relationship and constantly breathe new life into it.

Today, I see that I must invent our relationship each day. When I stop creating, our relationship loses its energy and its dynamics. But if I am present, if I create new possibilities each day, our relationship will grow.

December 9

Projects

"We imagined travelling around the world together. Our travel project was always a fundamental project in our relationship. We didn't know exactly when we'd be able to set out, but we were convinced that we'd do it one day. Finally, we had the chance to take a long trip and it lasted one whole year. It was wonderful! We visited more than 60 countries and we took over 5,000 photos. Now, at age 60, we're planning to live on a boat in the South Seas. What I like about our relationship is our desire to do things together and to share the same experiences."

— Emily B.

As a couple, we need to share projects. As we do, we can imagine our future and we can share our dreams. Planning shared projects gives us objectives we can reach together. Our projects can be grandiose or very simple. We can plan a weekend outing, a romantic dinner or a second honeymoon. Shared projects bring us closer and give us the opportunity to share experiences that enrich and strengthen our relationship.

Today, I plan projects with my partner. Life goes by so quickly and our day-to-day routines can be overwhelming. When we share projects, we give wings to our relationship.

December 10

Listening with Your Heart

"True love listens, aware that within the mystery of exchange we are united and that true exchange takes place not only in what we say but by what we hear profoundly. The mouth pronounces words, but the heart listens. And words remain in the heart — like a pebble thrown in a pond — leaving a lasting imprint in its very depths."

— Daphne Rose Kingma

Today, I listen with my heart. I close my ears to all meaningless background noise and I listen to the call of my heart, urging me to love and to get closer to my loved one. By listening with my heart, I can understand my partner and I can react to the needs in our relationship. By listening with my heart, I can see how important our relationship is and how it deserves to be protected and strengthened each and every day.

DECEMBER 11

Forget Routine!

The humdrum of everyday activities can be more harmful to a relationship than conflicts or misunderstandings. When we sink into a routine, we become like robots and we forget to make the gestures and say the words that keep our love alive. We can live with someone for years without truly creating a relationship. By breaking out of our everyday routine, we can reinvent the couple minute by minute and we can live in the present.

Today, I see that an everyday routine makes me feel secure. But I also see that our relationship must live and breathe. Each day I can invent moments of spontaneity to get closer to my partner. I can invent new activities and new projects so that our love and passion continues.

December 12

The Beauty Around Us

A relationship can be like a work of art. We can decide to build a beautiful relationship in a climate of harmony. Relationships that work well and that bring us pleasure and satisfaction are works of art that we create together with our partners. Communication can be positive, based on humor, pleasure and togetherness. Our activities can be pleasurable and can highlight our qualities and our sense of play. The places we frequent, principally our homes, can be places of tranquility and beauty. A relationship can be a work of art that we create together, day by day.

Today, I know that I can create a beautiful relationship with my partner.

DECEMBER 13

Clarifications

"I realized that my husband had changed. Early in our marriage, we did everything together. But gradually, he became more distant, much more involved in this job. I saw him briefly in the evening, when the children had gone to bed, but he preferred watching the news on television. On weekends, I had to argue to get him to organize an outing. I saw that we had to clarify things and I told him that things weren't going well between us. I told him that I wanted a dynamic relationship and if he couldn't do his fair share, then I would find someone else who was willing to show an interest in me. The conversation was like a slap in the face for him, it certainly opened his eyes. He is a changed man."

— GABRIELLA S.

A relationship is never static. The individuals in it evolve and change, and the relationship's dynamic change over time and with different circumstances. For these reasons, it may be necessary to clarify the situation from time to time. We must talk about the things that are important to us and we must describe exactly how we see things in our relationship. By going through this process periodically, our relationship grows and changes with us and can meet our needs and expectations of the moment.

Today, I no longer try to avoid clarifications. When I feel that we must talk, I don't wait.

DECEMBER 14

Being a Force for Peace

In a relationship, we can be the agent provocateur or we can be the force for peace. We can fuel arguments and conflicts or we can act in such a way as to restore calm. No one wins in a situation of conflict. When we are angry, we say and do things that we may regret in a few days or a few months. When we choose to be a force for peace, we quickly see that a conflict or an argument is something that is prepared. We remain calm and we react immediately to restore harmony. At times silence can be enough to avoid an escalation into conflict. At other times, we must use a more active method: for example, going out for a breath of fresh air. Each time we avoid a confrontation based on anger, we win. Anger is always a very poor mediator.

Today, I am a force for peace in our relationship. Anger, criticism and violence have no place in a relationship. Our objective is to help each other and not to argue or to punish each other. When I see a conflict on the horizon, I step back and I choose not to fuel it. By being calm and understanding, I can communicate without hurting.

DECEMBER 15

The Fear of Change

"When I told Albert that I wanted to go on a diet, he was thrilled. After the birth of our two children I had gained weight and I had 60 pounds to lose. I wanted to get back into the shape I was when we first met and I wanted to rekindle the passion between us. It took a lot of discipline to eat properly and to eliminate fat and sweets. I also started to go to an aerobic dance class to speed up the process. After three weeks, I'd lost 20 pounds and I was starting to feel really good about myself. That's when I began to realize that very subtly, Albert was trying to get me to drop the diet; he'd constantly offer me sweets and cakes. He wanted to sabotage me! When I confronted him, he denied it. He said that he didn't want me to make myself sick by dieting too much, but I could see that there was something else bothering him. He finally admitted that he was afraid to lose me if I managed to get my old figure back. If I stayed plump, men would be less attracted to me. I took the time to reassure him and I told him that he was the only man for me, he had nothing to fear."

— MARIE L.

Today, I see that I need not fear change. If I resist change, I am unhappy and I cannot enjoy our relationship to the fullest.

DECEMBER 16

Giving Support

In a relationship, one person's success is the other person's success. Each person must support the other in his or her projects. When a partner does good work, the relationship benefits. We are happy when we succeed in life. At work, in our families and in society, we seek success. Fortunately, success is possible when partners support each other. With support, we can find fulfillment and we can succeed in all aspects of life. Unfortunately, in many relationships there is a type of competition between the partners. They feel that one succeeds to the detriment of the other. But both can succeed and can share in each other's success, provided they give each other support and encouragement.

Today, I see that I have nothing to lose when I help my partner. I want to support my partner in all undertakings because I know that his or her success is also mine.

December 17

Freedom and Communication

A relationship requires a great deal of freedom and communication. We must know that we can spread our wings and pursue the goals we cherish while maintaining our relationship. We must have the ability to see our partner grow and we must be present in the relationship without imposing our views and without demanding that the other person give up his or her interests for the sake of the relationship. Verbal, emotional and spiritual communication must be the bond that keeps us together, each attuned to the other's reality. If effective communication prevails, we can be free and we can enjoy the stability and security of the relationship.

Today, I know that communication and freedom go hand in hand. A relationship should not be limiting. A relationship should contribute to our emotional and spiritual growth.

Making Our Partner Feel Secure

When we look closely at the motivations for building a relationship, we see that security is one of several important factors. When we refer to security, we do not necessarily mean financial security, although it does count. Rather, we mean the physical, moral, emotional and spiritual conditions that foster the stability and growth of each partner. In a good relationship, each person knows who they are, who they are with and where they are going. With the answers to these fundamental questions, we can function in society and we can reach most of our objectives.

Each partner has a role to play in creating a climate of security. By refusing to call the relationship into question needlessly and by accepting its legitimacy and its raison d'être, we contribute to this stability and security. Then, by being present in important moments, ready to provide our support and keep our word, we contribute to the climate of emotional security. And finally, by being honest and transparent in all our exchanges, we make the other person feel secure and we give them the support they need.

Today, I want to create a climate of stability and security in our relationship. I know the means that will help me create such a climate every day.

The Fundamental Being

My partner is searching for only one thing: a relationship with me. Me, the fundamental being. Our partner does not want a relationship with a mother, a sister, a best friend or the idea we have of who we are. Our partner sees something in us and so loves it that he falls in love. Where is the spontaneous and sincere person who couldn't hide her joy and her passion? Have I decided to save the real Me for a better use? We cannot be involved in a relationship if we wear a mask or if we present what we think of as an ideal facade. Our partner is in love with an authentic and vibrant being.

Today, I show my true colors. I know that I can be who I really am and I know that my partner loves me for who I am.

December 20

The Couple as a Spiritual Enterprise

A relationship is a spiritual undertaking that implies the involvement of two free and independent souls. Nothing determines our lives more than our choices. We are free to choose the life we will live. We are free to choose who we will build a relationship with and how long that relationship will last. We are free to agree or refuse to make a commitment to a relationship. Our choices shape what we are today and what we will become. Those who choose to build committed and long-term relationships will also have the advantage because they can take root and can show their true nature.

Today, I take root and I show my true nature.

DECEMBER 21

Surrounding Ourselves with Living Things

A relationship is alive and dynamic. We can ensure the survival, fulfillment and strength of our relationship by surrounding ourselves with living things: plants, animals, children, friends who have a positive outlook, the members of our extended family who want to contribute to our life together. By surrounding ourselves with living things, we avoid focusing our attention solely on ourselves and our relationship. We also feel the flow of strength and energy between two living beings.

Today, I seek living beings and things. Life seeks life. The dynamic strength of life spreads like fire and energizes all around it. So I surround my relationship with living beings and things.

DECEMBER 22

A Religious Philosophy

"I am one of those people who abandoned religious practice very young. I saw the Church as a scam based on outside appearances, something that had nothing to do with spirituality and everything to do with politics. I didn't feel that the Church had much to offer me and I couldn't identify with the God it offered me. As a child, however, I was very interested in the stories of the life Jesus led and the other stories in the Old Testament. As I got older, I started to feel an increasing need to find a religious philosophy that reflected my values. I often felt tormented and I had a lot of difficulty with relationships. By doing some research, I found the Buddhist religion (or religious and spiritual philosophy). This new perspective on life completely changed my way of living and saved my marriage. At last, I had a spiritual and moral framework to guide my decisions and to help me get through hard times."

— JOHN P.

Today, I know that I am a spiritual being and that the force that drives my relationship is a spiritual force. I must recognize this force in my life and I must live a positive life each day.

Recovering from a Breakup

We know that in North America, 50 percent of marriages end in divorce. We also know that couples avoid commitment, thinking that they can avoid the disastrous consequences of a breakup. A divorce or a breakup is a very painful experience. For a certain period of time, we experience painful emotions, we are confused and depressed. We often look unsuccessfully for the reason why the relationship ended. We are angry and bitter towards the person who dared to leave us, who turned our lives upside down and who destroyed our self-esteem and our morale.

For our own good and the good of those around us, we must recover as quickly as possible. By remembering to eat well, exercise, go out with friends, by staying away from drugs, alcohol and antidepressants, and by confiding in others, we can recover and smile again.

Today, I know that I will recover. I have a plan for recovery. I have a plan to free myself of negative emotions. I see that each day, I am getting better and better.

December 24

Refusing to Play Victim

Many individuals are convinced that they are victims. They feel that life and people have been particularly cruel and insensitive to them. They see their life as an unbelievable battle against adversity and they are always recovering from one defeat or another. They are convinced that life is extremely unfair to them personally. But the truth is that no one, if not ourselves, can make us a victim. We become victims because of our own perceptions and our own decisions.

Society attaches a great deal of importance and value to victimization. Our tax system and the way in which collective wealth is redistributed is based on the victimization of individuals. The reality is that there are people who choose to go beyond material conditions, whatever they may be, and there are others who seek to justify their lack of initiative and their fundamental incompetence.

Today, I see that the success of my relationship depends on me, on my actions and on my attitudes. I refuse to be a victim.

December 25

Being Together

Beyond its commercial value, Christmas Day is an opportunity to celebrate our relationship and our families. Beyond gifts, food, drinks and office parties, it is an occasion to be together and to enjoy ourselves together. Christmas is an opportunity to contact friends and family members and to be close to our partners.

Our hearts go out to those who find Christmas a difficult time as they look at their family, emotional and material situation. For many, Christmas is a day that brings back painful memories of breakups and alienation. We can hope that the divine light of Christmas shines down on them and helps them through their sadness.

Today, I am happy to be with my partner. I see that together, our life is better. I feel loved and I want to love and grow in our relationship.

December 26

Using Past Experiences

"After my divorce, I decided to use the things I had learned in our relationship to build a new and lasting relationship. I decided that I hadn't suffered in vain and that I was going to use my past experiences to build a good relationship. I saw that in my previous marriage, I had been unable to understand problems and to solve them. The partner I had chosen didn't want to improve the relationship. He was content with criticizing me and threatening me. My next partner will be more sensitive to the needs in the relationship and he will want to contribute to it."

— Jeanna D.

We can see the end of a relationship as a failure or as an experience we can learn from. We should not destroy ourselves by taking all the blame for the failure. Most probably, we did all we could with the resources and possibilities we had. What is important is to be ready to learn from our past experiences so that we can build a better future.

Today, I see that the end of a relationship is not the end of the world. I can recover and I can take stock of the situation. When I have, I can build a new relationship and I can use my past experiences as learning experiences.

December 27

Recognizing True Friends

"I believe that the friends we have as a couple helped us to overcome the crises we suffered. Fortunately, we were surrounded by people who cared for us. All of our close friends are couples. We all see each other frequently. They are the same age as us and they share similar realities. When John and I went through hard times and when our relationship was in doubt, our friends helped us and encouraged us to stay together and to overcome what stood between us. We're very happy that we decided to stay together. Without a support system, I think that we would have had a hard time weathering the storm."

— Teresa L.

An individual can be influenced by his or her environment. If the partners in a relationship are surrounded by single people, the result may be a negative influence on the relationship. Single people prefer to frequent single people who share their activities and interests. But if we surround ourselves with people who cherish our relationship and who share our values in life, we can count on their support when hard times come along.

Today, I make a conscious effort to choose friends who cherish our relationship. I believe in the value of a relationship.

December 28

Making Resolutions

We can make resolutions regarding our relationship. We can decide to practise more sports together and to enroll in fitness classes. We can decide to speak more gently and promise not to make negative comments or argue. We can decide to join a self-help group to end the dependencies that harm our relationship. A relationship is a precious asset that we must nurture and protect. Good resolutions aimed at strengthening our relationship will improve our quality of life. Some resolutions are harder to make than others. But by sharing our resolutions with our partners, we can find the support we need to reach our objectives.

Today, I begin to formulate resolutions for the new year. I know that by sharing my resolutions with my partner, I will achieve my objectives.

December 29

Sabotage

Some people envy our relationship. They would be happy to see us breaking up. For reasons I cannot understand, these people do not believe in love or commitment. They favor other alternatives: living single, extra-marital relationships, passing relationships with no commitment. Perhaps they have been hurt or perhaps their past relationships have ended badly and they do not want to see others succeed where they have failed. We must identify and eliminate the saboteurs in our lives.

A relationship is like a flowering plant. We must feed it and create all of the conditions it needs to grow and blossom. Saboteurs poison all those around them and they threaten the health of our relationship.

Today, I am vigilant. I see that some people do not believe in relationships. They can lead us to paths that harm our life and our happiness in our relationship. When I see a person like this in my environment, I take the means to remove him or her from my life.

Who Deserves a Good Relationship?

"When two individuals love each other from the depths of their souls, in addition to loving, desiring, cherishing, adoring and protecting each other, each is also the guardian and the protector of the well being of the other person's soul and ensures that the other person will make the decisions that foster the evolution of his or her soul. This may require the calm the soul thirsts for, the meditation that strengthens us, the prayer that soothes us. Turn away from the cacophony of the world and encourage the union of two souls."

— DAPHNE ROSE KINGMA

Today, I know that I deserve a positive relationship. I am not perfect by I want to love and I want to build a lasting relationship.

December 31

Preparing for the New Year

This is the dawn of a new year! As I look back, I see all the things we have experienced in the last twelve months. We have gone through hard times that tested our love. Fortunately, we have chosen to travel life together and to work at strengthening our relationship. We have had many more good times than bad times. I feel that we are closer today and that our relationship has matured. When I take stock, I see that my life is better within our relationship and that our efforts have been rewarded.

Today, I see that the new year marks the possibility of new experiences and new challenges. I can make the resolution of giving the best of myself to my partner. I look forward to our future and I know that we will succeed together.

PRINTED IN CANADA